THE AMERICAN SAILING ASSOCIATION'S

SAILING
MADE EASY

THE OFFICIAL MANUAL OF THE AMERICAN SAILING ASSOCIATION'S
BASIC KEELBOAT SAILING STANDARD (ASA101)

AMERICAN
SAILING
ASSOCIATION.

Produced for ASA by
Amanda Lunn Art Director
Damien Moore Editorial Director
Sharon Cluett, Sharon Rudd Art Editors
Jo Weeks Editor
Michael Forder Indexer

ASA would like to thank the following for their kind
permission to reproduce the following photographs:
page 6 top and center, Billy Black; page 7 top left and
right, Mike Kory; page 7 bottom, David Kory

First published by American Sailing Association in 2010

American Sailing Association
5301 Beethoven Street, Suite #265
Los Angeles, CA 90066

ISBN 978-0-9821025-0-3

Printed in the U.S.

Learning to Sail is Just the Beginning.

Become a member today and make your sailing
lifestyle richer. Let's sail off together on an incredibly fun
ASA flotilla, take a bareboating course, or let us help you
charter the boat of your dreams from one of ASA's
hundreds of worldwide affiliates. Scan here (or visit www.
asa.com) for more information on all the great benefits
that ASA membership has to offer.

visit us at
www.asa.com

CONTENTS

THE AMERICAN SAILING ASSOCIATION

The American Sailing Association was founded in 1983 with a simply stated mission: to teach people to sail safely and confidently. To achieve that goal, the ASA set out to establish standards against which to measure a sailor's level of knowledge and skill, the first such unified standards in the U.S. to apply to sailors in keelboats.

After studying programs offered in other countries, the founders of the ASA selected the Canadian Yachting Association's (CYA) "Learn to Cruise" program and licensed it for use in the U.S. With this strong heritage behind it, the ASA has continually improved and expanded its educational system by drawing on valuable input from the ASA school network.

Today, the ASA is an association of sailing schools, charter companies, professional sailing instructors, and sailors, with over 300 affiliated sailing schools located throughout the U.S., as well as in Europe, Japan, Central America, Taiwan, China, and other Far Eastern countries. These accredited schools offer ASA certification to individuals who meet the requirements for a given level.

The ASA system has eight primary levels of student certification. The newcomer begins at the ASA Basic Keelboat Standard (for which *Sailing Made Easy* serves as the textbook). Once he or she has passed the first course (requiring both a written exam and a practical on-the-water exam) the student receives the first level of certification and with it a seal for his or her personal *ASA Sailing Log Book* as proof of competence.

Whether your goal is to skipper a bareboat charter in the Caribbean or to crew confidently on a short weekend sail, the ASA's sailing-education system will guide you as you learn the theory behind sailing, practice the skills needed to handle a sailboat, and build the foundation of knowledge that will enable you to navigate a vessel safely and within the law.

By establishing national standards for sailing education, the ASA has provided a way for more people to take part in the sport safely, with the proper training and respect for their responsibilities as boaters, ensuring that sailing will be safer, smarter, and more fun for everybody.

For more information please visit our website at www.asa.com.

Charlie Nobles

ASA EXECUTIVE DIRECTOR

THE AIM OF THIS BOOK

While the primary purpose of *Sailing Made Easy* is to serve as the course book for the American Sailing Association (ASA) Basic Keelboat Sailing Standard, ASA101, it is designed to teach sailing to anyone, especially to those with little or no prior exposure to this exciting sport and lifestyle. In both these roles, it provides instruction in the skills and knowledge needed to competently sail a ballasted keelboat of up to about 25 feet in length in light to moderate winds.

When developing the content for this book, ASA drew on the experience gained by its instructors from the countless teaching hours they have accumulated on and off the water. It's no accident, therefore, that the text closely follows the normal sequence in which students are introduced to the theory of sailing, the boat in which they will take instruction, and the skills they will learn. On-the-water exercises demonstrate the theory and bring sailing to life while providing the student with the practice that builds confidence and promotes safety.

Sailing Made Easy also serves as the foundation of knowledge for subsequent ASA courses and their textbooks. Over half of ASA101 students continue on to ASA103, Coastal Cruising, where they build upon their basic sailing skills and are introduced to new topics, including engine use and anchoring. Those who progress to the next level of ASA104, Bareboat Cruising, master the skills required to charter and skipper a boat on a multi-day cruise — the goal of many novice sailors.

While this book is an excellent teaching tool for would-be sailors who want to learn by themselves, no text can substitute for the personal insights and individual attention an instructor can provide. For novice sailors embarking on a course of instruction at a sailing school, *Sailing Made Easy* provides valuable reading in advance of the course, support material during it, and a permanent reference to take on future sailing adventures. Review questions conclude four of the book's seven chapters to reinforce the information provided throughout the text and prepare the certificate-bound student for the ASA101 test.

Sailing has its own extensive vocabulary, and words and expressions that might be new to many readers pop up frequently in the text. Whenever a sailing-specific term appears for the first time, it is printed in *italic* and explained, very often with the help of an illustration. These words and some other common terms are also included in a glossary (see page 120).

THE ASA CERTIFICATION PROCESS

Congratulations! You are about to begin your ASA101 Basic Keelboat Sailing course.

Upon registration, your ASA sailing school will issue you an ASA Official Certification Logbook that includes all of the standards and a place for each certification seal you earn.

After you finish your sailing coursework, your instructor will administer a written exam to test your classroom knowledge, and an on-water exam to evaluate your sailing skills.

Upon successful completion, your instructor will immediately sign your logbook, and it will serve as proof of certification until you receive the ASA seal in the mail. The seal should be affixed in the logbook next to your instructor's signature. Remember to start logging your time on the water the next time you go sailing!

Your ASA certification includes a personalized membership card and a multitude of benefits that continue to expand each year. To see all of your great member benefits, go to ASA.com.

When you renew your membership each year, you will receive a new card with your updated certification levels printed on the back. Your membership card entitles you to valuable discounts and is also a great reminder that you received the best sailing education available!

SAIL AWAY WITH ASA...

Turn your sailing education into a fabulous life-changing vacation!

When you learn to sail with ASA, you're not only getting the best education, but also access to a lifetime of exploration, fun, and new friends by joining a community of people that share your passion for sailing.

Now that you are a sailor, you will think about getting on the water every opportunity you have! With that in mind, ASA schedules many exotic flotillas throughout the year, and you and your friends are invited to join us on these adventures. Once you have completed ASA104, Bareboat Cruising, you can look forward to skippering your own boat with family and friends in the destination of your dreams. You will soon realize that learning to sail is just the beginning of your adventure, and that you possess the knowledge and skills to sail safely and with confidence.

For the perfect flotilla or charter vacation for you, please visit ASA.com.

CONTRIBUTORS

ASA would like to acknowledge the contributions of the writers and editors who made this book possible.

EDITORS

Peter Isler is one of America's star professional sailors both on and off the water. At Yale University, he was named Collegiate Sailor of the Year and progressed from there to become involved in every America's Cup since 1987, when he was navigator aboard Dennis Conner's winning *Stars & Stripes*. In 2007, he sailed in his fifth Cup campaign serving as navigator for the BMW Oracle Racing Team. In the same period, he covered the America's Cup for three television networks. Peter co-authored the best-selling *Sailing for Dummies* and, as a director of ASA since 1983, has devoted a great deal of his time to bringing fresh faces into sailing.

Jeremy McGeary drifted off to sea from England in 1970 and, after five years working his way up from deckhand to skipper in the Caribbean yacht-charter fleet, drifted back ashore in 1975, in New England. Since then, he has built sailboats, designed them, and written about them for a fistful of publications — and done a little bit of sailing, too. A long freelance relationship with *Cruising World* magazine landed him a desk job in 1997 as an associate editor. Jeremy left *Cruising World* as senior editor in 2005 and now freelances as a writer and editor for several magazines.

Lenny Shabes is the founder of the American Sailing Association and is currently the Chairman of the Board. His first sailing experience was maneuvering a model boat on a lake in Central Park at age 8. Hooked for life, he has since raced and cruised around the world. He has been a boat broker, sailing instructor, and charter-boat captain. He has owned a sailing school and a charter company and has generally been involved in the marine industry for over 35 years. He and his wife, Cindy, currently own a J/100 that they race and day sail in Marina del Rey, California.

WRITERS

Harry Munns began sailing as a boy in his native Massachusetts. His love of the ocean took him to southern California where he began sailing, teaching, and working as a professional captain. He was one of the founders of the American Sailing Association, and in his 20-year career at ASA, Harry has trained hundreds of instructors around the world. He has written for and contributed to many boating publications and wrote the popular book, *Cruising Fundamentals*. He continues to sail, lecture, and write whenever time allows. Harry was the lead writer for this book.

Bob Diamond began his sailing career in the early 1970s when he was drafted as a sailing instructor at the summer camp where he was a counselor. From that time on, sailing became an obsession. After working as an elementary school teacher in San Jose, California, in 1984, Bob switched to teaching sailing full time at Spinnaker Sailing in Redwood City and has been a sailing instructor ever since. Bob is also a United States Coast Guard (USCG) licensed Master, and ASA Instructor Evaluator.

Tom Landers has been an avid sailor and charter captain for 40 years while cruising and racing on Chesapeake Bay. He has taught sailing professionally under ASA for over a decade and founded an ASA-certified sailing school in Deltaville, Virginia. Captain Tom has won several awards, as an ASA instructor, as an ASA school owner, and at the University of Richmond where he has taught sailing for many years. Because of his thorough knowledge of sailing, ASA selected him as the sailing-subject-matter expert for several sailing-related consulting projects.

Mary Swift-Swan began sailing in 1980 and a few years later decided that she wanted to teach sailing. She became a certified ASA instructor in 1985 and in the same year became a USCG licensed Captain. She opened her first sailing school in 1987 in Benicia, California, and worked with other schools to develop new programs, including courses for women. In 1997, Mary became the first woman ASA Instructor Evaluator. Today, she co-owns Afterguard Sailing Academy in Oakland with her husband, where they are developing an incentive program for high-schoolers.

Lan Yarbrough has been teaching ASA courses professionally since 1989 in places as far apart as Chesapeake Bay and the Nile River. While in Cairo, he was chief instructor for the Cairo Yacht Club and was nominated as a national sailing coach for Egypt. Lan, who had been sailing as long as he could remember, only got truly serious about it when he went to an ASA instructor for professional training and learned something new in every class. He is now a partner in Live and Learn Sailing, a California sailing school, where he indulges his great passion for teaching marine navigation in its traditional and electronic forms.

PHOTOGRAPHY

Bob Grieser was a photographer at the *Washington Star* for 15 years before joining the *LA Times*, where he stayed for 18 years. After a career covering news stories from riots, to war zones in Somalia, to White House events, he left the newsroom in 1998 for the unpredictable world of freelancing. A keen sailor, he takes assignments in the yachting, adventure, travel, and leisure industries.

ACKNOWLEDGEMENTS

ASA is also deeply grateful to the following people who have contributed their knowledge, guidance, and time to the realization of *Sailing Made Easy*:

Sarah Adams Consultant
Reed Freyermuth Founding Board Member
Charlie Nobles Executive Director

Jeff Riecks Instructor
Cynthia Shabes President
Brenda Wempner Education Coordinator

Thanks also to **Hunter Marine** for arranging the loan of the Hunter sailboats and **Peter Bull** for illustrations.

INTRODUCTION

The first time I sailed silently downwind on a warm summer's day, I knew I was in love. The feeling of being moved by the wind's power really stirred my soul and piqued my interest. I instantly understood that we were being pushed down the channel by the wind, but how would we get back? Was it possible to sail toward the wind? I immediately wanted to know everything I could about this magical new pastime.

That was 35 years ago, and today, every time I go sailing, I still learn something new that makes me a better sailor. This book is the first step in a voyage that will last you the rest of your life. It is a gift from a group of dedicated sailing professionals who have committed their lives to sharing their art, their skill, and their passion for this wonderful activity. You are just embarking on this same journey. You may become a cruiser or a racer, you might not venture farther than your local harbor, or maybe you will sail around the world, but one thing is for sure, your life will be enriched by sailing.

Fair Winds

Lenny Shabes

ASA CHAIRMAN OF THE BOARD

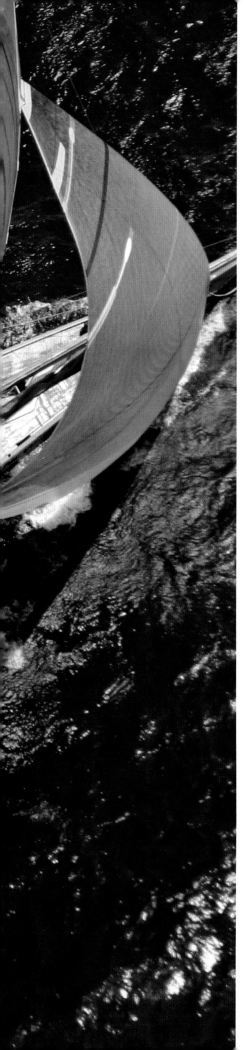

FOREWORD

"There is nothing — absolutely nothing —
half so much worth doing as simply
messing about in boats."

Water Rat to Mole, in Kenneth Grahame's classic, *The Wind in the Willows*

When you learn how to sense the wind and harness its power to move your boat, a whole new world opens up before you. Whichever way the wind then blows you, whatever course you choose to take in this diverse sport, you will find rich rewards.

You may be drawn toward the challenge and adventure of cruising to new harbors, following in the wakes of seafarers whose voyages changed the course of civilization. You may get bitten by the sailboat racing bug. Or you may simply relish magical stolen moments spent gliding over the waves, at one with nature, cast off, if only for a few hours, from shore-side cares.

By opening this book you are taking a concrete first step toward becoming a sailor and realizing your dream of a nautical future. Many paths lead into this great sport, just as many types of boat await to be sailed, but when the time comes to get serious about your sailing education, the American Sailing Association (ASA) is an ideal first port of call.

Over the past several decades, hundreds of thousands of people have learned to sail at ASA schools. By taking your first cues from an ASA certified instructor, learning from ASA manuals, and following a curriculum and graduated set of internationally recognized Standards, you too can go from beginner to "old salt" qualified to prepare a sailboat and skipper it across an ocean. By learning at an ASA school and becoming certified to ASA Standards, you will be assured that the fundamental building blocks in your sailing education are as solid as the keel on a seaworthy boat.

But what you learn in the pages of this book and from your ASA certified instructor is just the beginning. To really become a sailor you must take that knowledge out on the water and practice using it to build up your experience. In the process, beware: Like many before you, you may become hooked to a lifetime of fun messing about in boats!

Peter Isler

TWO-TIME AMERICA'S CUP-WINNING NAVIGATOR

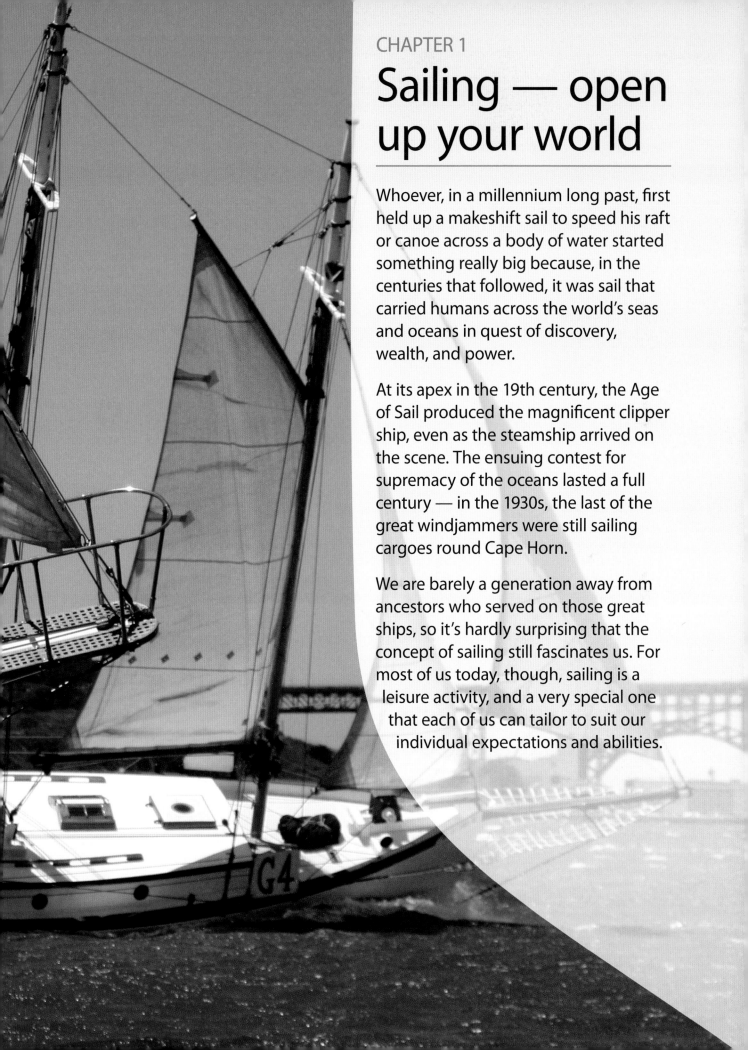

CHAPTER 1

Sailing — open up your world

Whoever, in a millennium long past, first held up a makeshift sail to speed his raft or canoe across a body of water started something really big because, in the centuries that followed, it was sail that carried humans across the world's seas and oceans in quest of discovery, wealth, and power.

At its apex in the 19th century, the Age of Sail produced the magnificent clipper ship, even as the steamship arrived on the scene. The ensuing contest for supremacy of the oceans lasted a full century — in the 1930s, the last of the great windjammers were still sailing cargoes round Cape Horn.

We are barely a generation away from ancestors who served on those great ships, so it's hardly surprising that the concept of sailing still fascinates us. For most of us today, though, sailing is a leisure activity, and a very special one that each of us can tailor to suit our individual expectations and abilities.

SAILING — THE WHAT, THE HOW, AND THE WHERE

Few activities offer such a variety of pleasures as sailing. Something special happens when you cast off from shore, leaving your land-based cares behind, and sail away under the power of mother nature. And while technology has brought great advances in the design of sailboats and their gear, much of the satisfaction derived from sailing comes as a sensation, feeling the boat as it responds to your actions and to the force of the wind and waves. Sailing a boat well is part art and part skill, but whichever side of the brain is engaged at any moment, one key element is always up front and central, and that's the wind.

WIND, THE CENTER OF THE SAILOR'S UNIVERSE

Wind is the sailor's fuel, and "knowing" the wind and its direction relative to your boat and sails is a critical element in learning to sail. Because the wind dictates how and where you can sail, you need to be constantly aware of its speed and direction. As a new sailor, nothing is more important to you than increasing your sensitivity to the wind. Learn to watch for wind's "clues" — the ripples and waves on the water, other sailboats, flags, smoke, anything affected by the breeze so that you become as aware of the wind as a bird.

We feel the wind and can intuitively understand how a sail can help move a boat along in the same direction the wind is blowing. But how do we achieve more control over our sailboat than over a leaf being pushed along by the wind?

The leaf offers no resistance to the wind, and is at its mercy. A sailboat is immersed in water, which grips it and allows it to resist the force of the wind. By playing the force of the wind on a sail against the resisting force of the water against the hull, we can harness the wind's energy to drive a modern sailboat virtually anywhere we want to go.

SAILS AND THE WIND

The earliest sailboats had primitive sails that were only useful when the destination the sailors wanted to go was *downwind*, or the direction the wind was blowing toward. If the destination was *upwind*, in the direction the wind was blowing from, the sailors had to resort to oars or paddles, or wait until the wind changed.

Even a simple sail can be moved into different positions relative to the boat, and this allows even a fairly primitive sailboat to sail at an angle to the wind, albeit still in a downwind direction.

As techniques and technology developed, so did the design of sailing vessels. At the dawn of the Age of Sail, in the 16th century, large ships could sail quite effectively across the wind.

Oriented to the wind in this way, even an old-time square sail begins to take on the characteristics of an *airfoil*.

AIRFOILS AND SAILS

An airfoil is an object designed to take advantage of the energy of the wind by deflecting or bending the wind without greatly disturbing its flow. Wind passing across the airfoil creates both *lift*, a desired force, and *drag*, a hindering force. Birds have been using airfoils for a long time and adjust the angle and spread of their wings according to whether they want to soar (using lift) or slow down for a landing (using drag). Airplane wings exploit similar shapes but with less versatility, and the mechanism by which a modern sail generates a driving force is analogous to how an airplane's wing allows it to fly — they are both acting as airfoils.

To get an idea of how a sail creates lift, hold your hand out of the window of a moving car. When you hold your hand vertically, so your palm faces the wind,

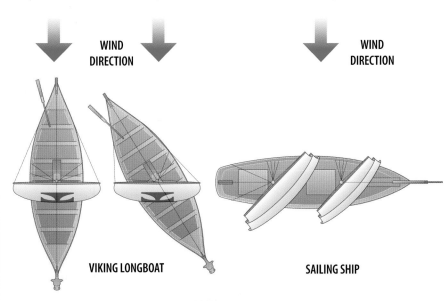

WIND DIRECTION

WIND DIRECTION

VIKING LONGBOAT

SAILING SHIP

A simple sail drove a Viking longboat downwind, limiting the occasions on which the sail was useful. Setting the sail at an angle to the boat opened up a wider range of courses it could sail, but all were still downwind.

Sailing ships sailed across the wind helped by deep hulls that resisted being pushed sideways.

the wind pushes it backwards — your hand is like the square sail on the longboat, with the wind simply pushing against it. Now, slowly rotate your hand so the top of it inclines forward. You will start to feel the wind trying to lift it. Your hand is now redirecting some of the force of the wind to create lift.

In both cases, you have to exert force to prevent your hand from being blown backwards. The comparable "backwards" force on a sailboat is counteracted by the resistance provided by the boat pushing on the water. In fact, when the boat is moving, the parts of it under the water are doing their own "lifting" too. More on that later.

SAILING TOWARD THE WIND

Even when a few centuries ago sailors learned about the airfoil effect (although they didn't call it that yet), the design of their boats and their sails, and the materials available for putting them

together, limited their capabilities. They could sail downwind and across the wind, but achieving any significant progress toward the wind was impossible. That left half a circle of directions toward which they could not sail until the wind changed.

Over the years, advances in knowledge and technology have enabled us to further exploit the principle of lift, both above the water in sails and below the water in refined designs of keels and rudders. With these improvements, modern sailboats have reduced this *no-sail zone*, where it's impossible to make forward progress, to about 90 degrees — 45 degrees on either side of the wind — or even less. So today, the wind's direction no longer limits where a sailboat can travel. It can sail directly toward any destination except one in the no-sail zone, and to reach a destination in that region, a sailor simply sails a zig-zag course of two or more legs to get there.

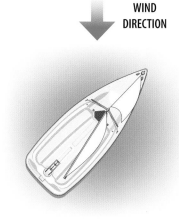

WIND DIRECTION

No-sail zone

A modern sailboat can sail as close as 45 degrees to the direction from which the wind is blowing.

It's no accident that sails and a bird's wing are similar in appearance: they are both airfoils.

THE POINTS OF SAIL

As we've seen, it's the direction of the wind that dictates the direction a sailboat can sail. It's hardly surprising, then, that sailors orient themselves according to the wind and describe the direction a sailboat is going as it relates to the wind. To become a sailor, you have to understand these terms, illustrated in the Points of Sail diagram which depicts the range of courses a sailboat can and cannot travel — all oriented relative to the wind.

COURSES AND THE WIND

Imagine the face of a clock where the wind is blowing straight down from 12 o'clock and the boat is sitting in the middle. At the top, from about 10:30 to 1:30 (depending on your boat and the wind speed) is the no-sail zone. It is physically impossible for a boat to sail directly toward any direction within that roughly 90-degree zone. If you try, the sails begin to flap, losing their power, and the boat will come to a halt.

At either edge of the no-sail zone are the two *close-hauled* courses, so called because the sails are hauled as close to the boat's centerline as they will go. As the boat's course turns away from the wind, it enters a zone called *reaching*, where the wind is coming across the boat. Reaching is such a broad zone that we divide it up into three parts: *beam reaching* when the boat is sailing at 90 degrees to the wind, *close reaching* as the course gets closer to close-hauled, and *broad reaching* when the boat's heading is farther down the face of our clock. If a boat is sailing directly away from the wind, toward 6 o'clock

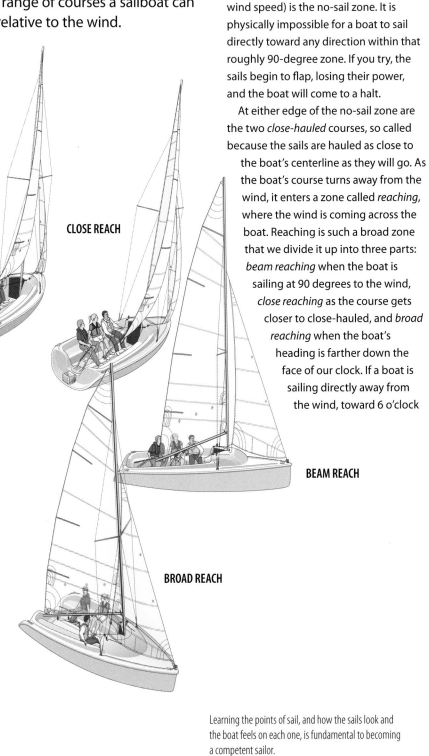

WIND
DIRECTION

IN IRONS

CLOSE-HAULED

CLOSE REACH

No-sail
zone

Close-hauled

Close reach

12

3

Beam reach

9

6

Broad reach

Run

BEAM REACH

BROAD REACH

RUN

Learning the points of sail, and how the sails look and the boat feels on each one, is fundamental to becoming a competent sailor.

(or within a few minutes of it), it is *running* or sailing *downwind*.

On each of these points of sail, the sails have to be set or *trimmed* differently to gain optimum thrust from the wind. Each course also has its corresponding technique for steering.

TRIMMING THE SAILS

Without any means of controlling it, a sail would simply flap in the wind like a flag. To capture the wind's energy, it must be positioned so that the air flows around it smoothly. Every time the boat's angle to the wind changes, the sail *trim* should change too. That is, the sail's relative angle to the wind must be adjusted so that it works as an airfoil at its highest efficiency — producing maximum lift. You trim a sail by means of lines (the sailor's term for nearly all rope on a boat) or wires attached to the sail or to its *boom*, a spar attached to the bottom of the sail.

APPARENT WIND

The wind that you feel on a moving sailboat, and to which you steer and trim the sails, has a different direction and speed than the wind your friend feels standing on the dock that you are sailing past.

Picture yourself riding a bicycle. Even on a calm day, you feel a "wind" on your face — the effect of your movement through the still air. On a windy day, you feel the wind more strongly when you ride toward it than when riding away from it. In each case, you are feeling the *apparent wind*, which is a combination of the *true wind* (that you feel when standing still) and the wind that you create by virtue of your own motion through the air. Whenever a sailboat is moving, the wind that you feel, and that is hitting the sails, is the apparent wind, so it's the apparent wind that governs how a boat sails. But since the apparent wind is the only wind you ever feel on a boat when it's moving, there's really nothing tricky about it at all — just feel the wind and steer and trim your sails accordingly.

The masthead fly shows the direction of the apparent wind. This one is indicating the boat is sailing on a beam reach.

MASTHEAD FLY

The masthead fly is a small wind vane at the top of the mast that shows the direction from which the apparent wind is coming. Look at the masthead fly to determine what point of sail you are on so you can trim your sails correctly to the course you want to steer. If the arrow's tail is inside the vee formed by the two arms, you are in the no-sail zone (see the wind rose on page 18).

WIND DIRECTION

Apparent wind 13 knots

True wind 10 knots

45°

33°

Boat speed 4 knots

CLOSE-HAULED

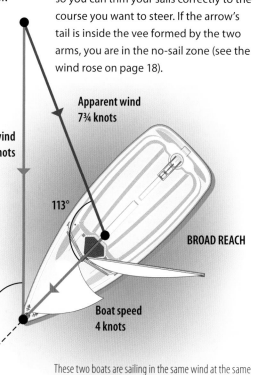

Apparent wind 7¾ knots

True wind 10 knots

113°

135°

Boat speed 4 knots

BROAD REACH

These two boats are sailing in the same wind at the same speed. Aboard the close-hauled boat, sailing toward the wind, the apparent wind is stronger than the true wind. Aboard the broad-reaching boat, which is sailing away from the wind, the apparent wind has much less strength.

ANATOMY OF A SAILBOAT

THE LANGUAGE OF THE SEA — SAILOR SPEAK

Over the centuries, sailing has acquired a lexicon and a language of its own. When their seafaring days were done, sailors returned to the land, often to regions far from the ocean. As a consequence, nautical terms, many of them with foreign origins, have become part of our general vocabulary. Part of learning to sail is learning its language. All you need to begin with are a few fundamental terms; the rest will attach themselves like barnacles the more time you spend sailing.

NAMING PARTS OF A BOAT

Underlying every watercraft, from a lowly rowboat on a lake to the mightiest aircraft carrier, is the *hull*, the watertight floating body of the boat that gives it form and houses or supports every other part of the boat. Hulls fall into an infinity of shapes and sizes, each related to its purpose and design heritage.

When learning to sail, the type of boats you will most likely encounter will be dinghies and keelboats.

A *dinghy* is a small sailboat, usually under 20 feet long and open for most of its length.

A *keelboat* is usually larger, starting at about 20 feet and with no apparent upper length limit — some megayachts are over 200 feet long.

The key difference, other than size, is that a keelboat has a *keel*, a fixed appendage on the bottom of the hull that provides the sideways resistance needed to counter the force of the wind on the sails. The keel also carries *ballast*, usually iron or lead, the weight of which counteracts the force of the wind that causes a sailboat to *heel*, or lean over. On a modern boat, the keel is shaped in the form of an airfoil wing to generate lift, which helps it sail closer to the wind.

A dinghy has neither a keel nor ballast. To resist sideways movement it has a *centerboard* or a *daggerboard* that can be lowered or raised as needed. A centerboard pivots up and down within its trunk; a daggerboard slides up and down vertically. To resist heeling, sailing dinghies use live ballast — the crew sitting out on the edge of the boat. Many kids learn to sail at yacht clubs and in community programs aboard these smaller craft which are very responsive to changes in wind and trim and placement of (human) ballast. Errors can result in *capsize*, or tipping over — all part of the appeal to youngsters.

Multihulls, boats with more than one hull, have their origins in the craft used by indigenous Pacific islanders. Their distant descendants, modern *catamarans* (two hulls) and *trimarans* (three hulls), can be very fast or very roomy, depending on whether they have been designed for speed or comfort.

A sailboat is steered by a fin-shaped *rudder*, attached beneath the boat toward the stern, which can be rotated to change the angle at which the water strikes it. The rudder won't work when the boat is at rest; it needs the flow of water past the moving boat to create the force to turn the boat. On dinghies and small keelboats, the rudder is operated by means of the *tiller*, a long lever attached to its top. Most bigger boats employ a steering wheel, which controls the rudder angle through a series of gears, cables, and pulleys. Whether wheel or tiller, it's also the *helm*, and the person steering the boat is the *helmsman*.

Just because there has to be an exception to every general rule, a type of boat exists that has no rudder. A

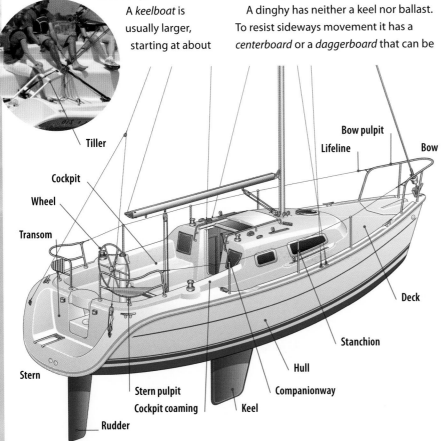

Tiller

Cockpit

Wheel

Transom

Stern

Stern pulpit

Cockpit coaming

Rudder

Keel

Companionway

Hull

Stanchion

Deck

Bow pulpit

Lifeline

Bow

sailboard is, at its root, a surfboard with a sail. Its sailor steers it by trimming the sail and shifting his body weight.

INTRODUCING THE KEELBOAT

As you can see, variety is ubiquitous in the world of sailboats and their designs. That's one of the aspects of our sport that makes it appealing to so many different people. And the variations don't end with the hull shapes and underwater fins. There is no single best type of boat. As you gain more experience, you may find yourself being drawn to a particular type suited to your home waters, your personality, or your dreams. Maybe you'll decide to sail the world on a tall ship, or attempt to break the world sailing-speed record skimming across shallow water at speeds well over 55 mph on a board powered by a kite.

Wherever your sailing takes you, you begin by learning the same principles, and in *Sailing Made Easy* we'll focus on the 20- to 30- foot modern keelboats commonly used in sailing schools. These boats are small and responsive enough to provide the new sailor with the feel and feedback that is so important when learning, but big and stable enough to carry an instructor and the students in comfort.

Unlike a dinghy, a keelboat won't capsize. In a strong wind it may heel a long way over, but the ballast in its keel is designed to keep it from capsizing. And while sailing either type of boat can be exciting, learning to sail in a keelboat is more relaxing than doing so in a dinghy. So we continue our tour of sailing terminology with a small keelboat as our model, but most of these basic terms apply to all types of sailboats.

As a safety feature, most keelboats not used exclusively for racing are fitted with *lifelines*. Usually made of wire cable, they run around the perimeter of the deck and about two feet above it, supported by *stanchions*. At the bow and stern, the lifelines are attached to tubular-metal frameworks called *pulpits*.

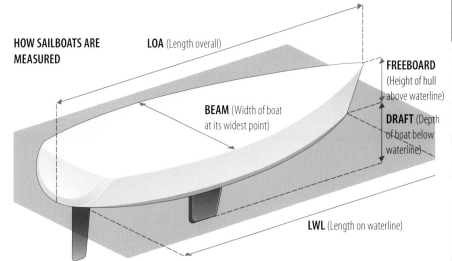

HOW SAILBOATS ARE MEASURED

LOA (Length overall)

FREEBOARD (Height of hull above waterline)

BEAM (Width of boat at its widest point)

DRAFT (Depth of boat below waterline)

LWL (Length on waterline)

Sailboats are commonly compared by LOA. LWL is used to estimate maximum sailing speed—longer is faster. A boat's draft dictates the minimum depth of water in which it can sail. Freeboard is usually less at the stern than at the bow.

A typical modern keelboat has a ballast keel shaped like a stubby aircraft wing and a deep, narrow rudder, both of which have airfoil shapes. The darker color shows the shape of the hull under the water.

A multihull, whether a two-hulled catamaran or a three-hulled trimaran, gains its resistance to heeling from its width. Because these boats don't need ballast, they can be very light and therefore fast.

A dinghy is a small, open boat that has no keel or fixed ballast — its crew balance the boat by moving their weight into or away from the center. Dinghy sailing can be exhilarating and wet.

WHERE'S WHERE ON AND OFF A SAILBOAT

Just as we divide our world into north, south, east, and west to establish where we are on it and where we're going, sailors have ways to describe locations on and around the smaller world of a boat. Some of the terms used are so ancient they refer to structural features that no longer even appear on boats. Others, of course, are related to the wind.

ONBOARD ORIENTATION

The front, or *forward* end of a boat is called the *bow* while the back, or *aft* end, is the *stern*. Forward and aft are also directions: From wherever you happen to be on the boat, anything between you and the bow is forward of you; anything between you and the stern is aft of you.

Many hulls end at the stern in a flat panel called the *transom*. As we have seen, the rudder is at or near the stern, and quite often hung from the transom. The area around and just forward of the tiller or steering wheel, where the crew performs most boat handling operations, is called the *cockpit*.

The sides of the hull, from the edge of the deck down to the water are the *topsides*. A boat is said to have low *freeboard* if the topsides are low relative to the boat's length. An oil tanker, for example, has low freeboard when full and high freeboard when empty.

Sailors have their own words to define right and left as related to the boat. The right-hand side of the boat when you are facing forward is the *starboard* side; the left-hand side is the *port* side. Forward and aft and port and starboard are definitive. They do not change even if the boat is moving backwards, or *going astern*.

Port and starboard are also used to describe locations of areas and objects off the boat relative to the boat. You might spot another boat *off the starboard bow*, for example.

An object sighted *abeam*, is positioned at roughly a right angle to the boat's centerline. (A *beam* is a structural member that crosses a ship from side to side, hence "across the beam" became "abeam.") Anything sighted aft of the beam, if it's not directly *astern*, will be off the port or starboard *quarter*.

When sailing, you'll encounter two more terms, *windward* and *leeward*, that are also used to specify directions. Like so much in sailing, these relate to the wind direction. Windward means toward the wind, so the side of the boat upon which the wind is blowing is the windward side. Leeward (pronounced loo'ard) means away from the wind, so the leeward side of the boat is the downwind side. If you are looking out over the starboard side of your boat and the wind is in your face, the starboard side is the windward side. The other side is the leeward side. Sometimes the term *weather* is used instead of windward, and *lee* instead of leeward. Either the port or the starboard side might be the windward side, but if you're aware, as any sailor should be, of where the wind is, when the lookout calls "Land ho! Off the windward bow," you'll know where to look.

On a small keelboat, much of the area aft of the mast is usually given over to the cockpit. Forward, under the deck, is space that can be used to store sails, equipment and personal gear. On bigger boats, the interior space formed between the hull and deck (often raised in the center to provide more room) is usually fitted out with living quarters, and sometimes divided into multiple *cabins*. Access below decks is via an opening called the *companionway* that is usually protected from the weather by a companionway *hatch*.

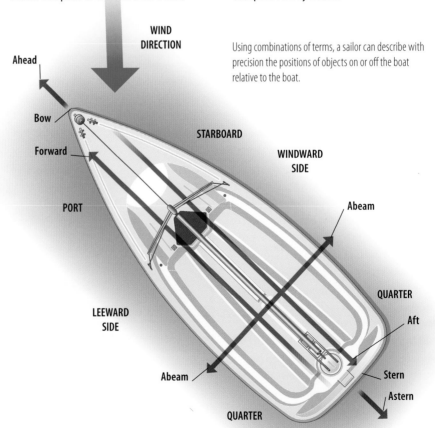

Using combinations of terms, a sailor can describe with precision the positions of objects on or off the boat relative to the boat.

WIND DIRECTION

Ahead

Bow

Forward

PORT

STARBOARD

WINDWARD SIDE

Abeam

LEEWARD SIDE

QUARTER

Aft

Abeam

Stern

Astern

QUARTER

CAPTURING THE WIND — SAILS, SPARS, AND RIGGING

The wind's energy, captured by the sails, provides the driving force for a sailboat. To be effective, sails must be rigged so that they can be trimmed to present the most efficient wing shape to the wind — according to the direction you want to go. The entire system of sails, spars, and associated rigging comprises the sailboat's rig.

SPARS

A *spar* is a pole of any type used to support the sails. Our small keelboat has two spars: the *mast*, which stands vertically from the deck and supports the sails, and the *boom*, which supports the bottom edge of the *mainsail*, the aftmost sail. Together they help to spread the sails to the wind. The boom is connected to the mast by an articulated connection called a *gooseneck*. While some boats are still rigged with wooden spars and on others they are made of carbon fiber, aluminum is the material most commonly used today.

THE SAILS

Our generic keelboat is rigged as a *sloop* — the most common of sail plans. A sloop has one mast and (usually) just two sails: the mainsail, which has its forward edge attached to the mast, and a *headsail*. Headsail is a generic term that refers to any sail that sets forward of the mast and our sloop-rigged keelboat features the most common one, the *jib*. A jib that is so big it overlaps the mast can be called a *genoa*. A genoa is best suited to light and moderate winds, and in strong winds might be replaced by a smaller jib made of stronger fabric.

PARTS OF A SAIL

All sails share common names for their edges and corners. The *luff* is a sail's forward edge; it feels the wind first. The luff of the mainsail is usually hoisted up and attached to the mast. The luff of the jib is attached to the *forestay* (we'll get to this and other parts of the rigging shortly). When a sail is trimmed correctly, and acting like a wing, wind flows smoothly across it from the luff to the *leech*, the sail's back edge. The bottom edge of a sail is called the *foot*. Between the luff and the foot at the sail's bottom front corner is the *tack*. Whenever a sail is in use, the tack is securely attached to the boat or to a spar; if it weren't, you'd have no control over the sail. The corner at the very top of the sail, between the luff and the leech, is the *head*. This corner, too, remains fixed, supported by the mast and its rigging when the sail is working. The third corner of our triangle, between the leech and the foot, is the *clew*. The control lines connected to a sail's clew allow you to make the most important adjustments to its trim.

Because the leech of the mainsail is unsupported along its entire length, sailmakers employ *battens*, solid slats or rods, to help maintain the desired airfoil shape. The battens, which may extend partially or all the way from the leech to the luff, are usually made of fiberglass or wood and are held in *batten pockets* stitched to the surface of the sail. Less commonly, battens are also employed in a jib.

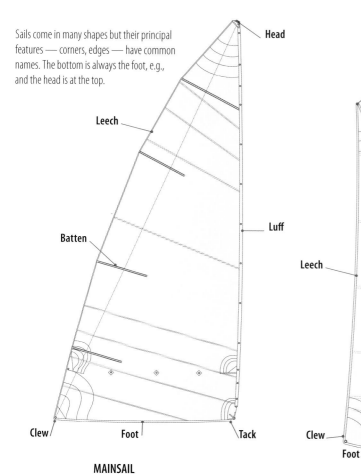

Sails come in many shapes but their principal features — corners, edges — have common names. The bottom is always the foot, e.g., and the head is at the top.

Head

Leech

Luff

Batten

Clew **Foot** **Tack**

MAINSAIL

Head

Luff

Leech

Clew
Foot **Tack**

JIB

STANDING RIGGING

To remain solid and upright under the loads imposed by the sails, boat, and wind, the mast needs support. This is the job of the *standing rigging*, so called because it remains fixed in place even when no sails are set. A plethora of systems is employed for standing rigging but we'll focus on our model keelboat.

Standing rigging is commonly made up of wire cables. Those holding the mast in its fore-and-aft position are called *stays*. The *backstay* runs from the top of the mast to the stern; the *forestay* or *headstay* runs from the top of the mast, or near the top, to the bow. Many boats have *roller furling*, where the luff of the jib is attached to a foil-shaped tube that encloses the forestay. This is a very convenient system because when not in use, the jib is easily put away by rolling it around the forestay with the aid of a spool (the *roller furler*) at the bottom of the forestay.

Shrouds provide sideways support for the mast. They are fixed to the sides of the mast at or near its top (on taller masts there can be several levels of shrouds) and run down to the outer edge of the deck to strong fittings called *chainplates*. To create a more effective angle of support, shrouds are sometimes pushed farther away from the mast by strong struts called *spreaders*.

TIP *Sailors recognize fellow sailors by how they pronounce certain words. You've already met leeward (pronounced loo'ard). Now would be a good time to start saying mains'l and heads'l.*

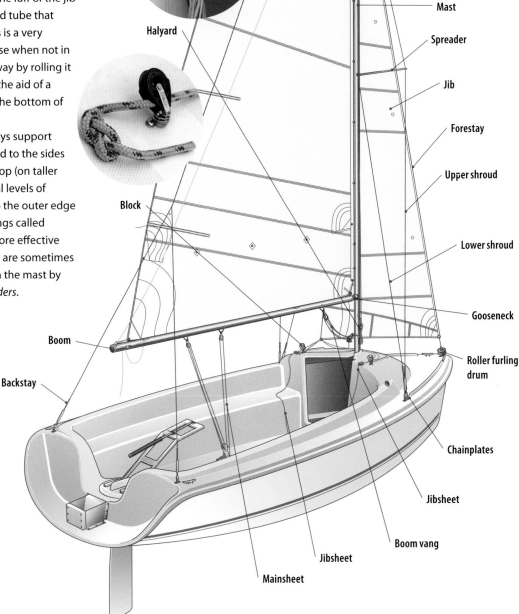

Masthead

Boom topping lift

Mainsail

Halyard

Block

Boom

Backstay

Mast

Spreader

Jib

Forestay

Upper shroud

Lower shroud

Gooseneck

Roller furling drum

Chainplates

Jibsheet

Boom vang

Jibsheet

Mainsheet

This small keelboat, about 20 feet long is rigged as a sloop: one mast, two sails. Most of the named parts are found on sailboats of all sizes and rigs.

RUNNING RIGGING — A ROPE BY ANY OTHER NAME…

Where the standing rigging remains fixed and is adjusted only rarely to ensure that the mast is properly supported, the ropes used to control the trim and shape of the sails are constantly being worked when sailing, and are called the *running rigging*.

> **TIP** *Be very careful what you call a rope on a boat. To a sailor, rope is a raw material. A piece of rope that does a job is called a line, and every line has a name.*

A *halyard* is a line used to raise or hoist a sail. It attaches to the head of the sail and runs over a pulley at the top of the mast (or in the case of a jib, near where the forestay joins the mast). You hoist a sail by pulling on the part of the halyard that returns downward to the deck.

A *sheet* is the primary line that controls the trim of a sail because it sets the angle of the sail relative to the flow of the wind (remember your hand hanging out of the car window?). A sheet is usually named for the sail that it controls (e.g. *jibsheet*). The jibsheets (there are two, one for each side of the boat) usually attach directly to the sail's clew (you'll learn the knot to use later in the book). In the case of the mainsail, the *mainsheet* is usually attached via a system of pulleys to the aft end of the boom.

Pulleys are used in great numbers on a sailboat, but sailors call them *blocks*. Blocks can be combined in many ways to increase your pulling power, or *purchase*. In a *block and tackle*, a line runs through a series of blocks arranged to multiply the force applied to the end of the line.

Such a block and tackle is often used for the *boom vang*, which restrains the boom from being lifted upward by the mainsail when the mainsheet is slackened.

Sheeting systems vary between boats, but it's quite common for the mainsheet to run through more blocks attached near deck level to a *traveler*. The traveler is made up of a track that runs across the cockpit or the deck and carries a movable *car* to which the sheet is attached.

When the mainsail is raised, it holds up the boom. To support the boom when the sail isn't set, some boats are rigged with a rope or wire, called a boom *topping lift* or boom lift, that runs from the top of the mast to the aft end of the boom.

Once we get aboard, we'll get into the all important techniques for sail trim, and all these names will begin to make a lot more sense.

ADVANCED SAILING

Sailing a keelboat downwind in light winds under just a mainsail and jib can be slow going. In such conditions, a huge lightweight balloon-shaped headsail called a *spinnaker* can bring back the excitement. These specialty downwind sails and much more await you as you build your sailing skills. But for now as you begin to learn to sail, it's important to focus on the basics with just a mainsail and jib.

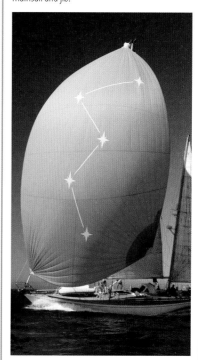

A FAMILY OF SHACKLES

A *shackle* is a fastening device used to connect lines or wire cables to an item of hardware. It's commonly in the shape of a D, the straight side of which is a rod that passes through a ring at one end of the D and threads into the other. Shackles come in a variety of other shapes and configurations and in all sizes. Some, like the halyard shackle, are designed for specific purposes. You should learn how to unsnap or unscrew every shackle on your boat. Shackles need to be well tightened, and a *shackle key* is a useful tool to keep handy both for tightening and undoing shackle pins.

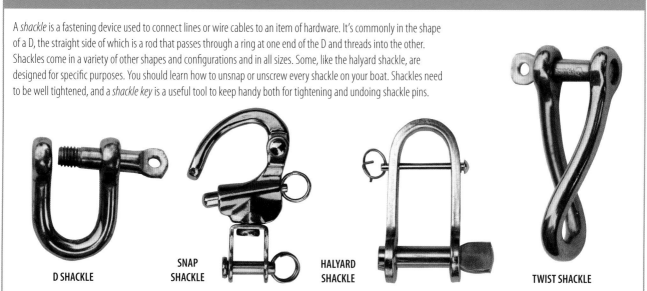

D SHACKLE   SNAP SHACKLE   HALYARD SHACKLE   TWIST SHACKLE

REVIEW QUESTIONS (see page 126 for answers)

FILL IN THE BLANK OR MATCH THE LETTER WITH THE WORD

1 When sailing, always be aware of the wind's _____ and _____.

2 The desirable force generated by the wind moving across a sail is called _____.

3 The direction relative to the wind in which the sailboat cannot sail is called the _____ _____ _____.

4 Sailboats can reach an upwind destination by sailing a _____ course.

5 The point of sail at the edge of the no-sail zone is called _____ _____.

6 A boat sailing across the wind is said to be _____.

7 Sailing straight downwind is called _____.

8 As the sailboat's direction changes relative to the wind, so should the sail's _____ to the wind be adjusted.

9 The combination of the true wind and the wind created by the boat's motion (that we feel on the boat) is called _____ wind.

10 The _____ is an underwater fin fixed on the bottom of the sailboat that provides stability and lateral resistance.

11 The sailboat's direction through the water is controlled by the _____, which can be turned by means of either a _____ or a _____ _____.

For Questions 12 through 15, identify the named parts with the lettered items in the diagrams:

12 Parts of a Sailboat	**13** The Sailboat's Rig	**14** Parts of a Sail	**15** On-Board Orientation
☐ Hull	☐ Mast	☐ Head	☐ Port
☐ Deck	☐ Boom	☐ Tack	☐ Starboard
☐ Cockpit	☐ Gooseneck	☐ Clew	☐ Forward
☐ Transom	☐ Spreader	☐ Luff	☐ Aft
☐ Bow	☐ Shroud	☐ Leech	☐ Ahead
☐ Stern	☐ Headstay/Forestay	☐ Foot	☐ Abeam
☐ Rudder	☐ Backstay	☐ Batten	☐ Astern
☐ Helm	☐ Mainsail		☐ Windward
☐ Stanchion	☐ Headsail/Jib		☐ Leeward
☐ Lifeline	☐ Halyard		
☐ Pulpit	☐ Mainsheet		
	☐ Jibsheet		
	☐ Boom Vang		
	☐ Boom Topping Lift		

12 Parts of a Sailboat

13 The Sailboat's Rig

14 Parts of a Sail

15 On-Board Orientation

WIND
DIRECTION

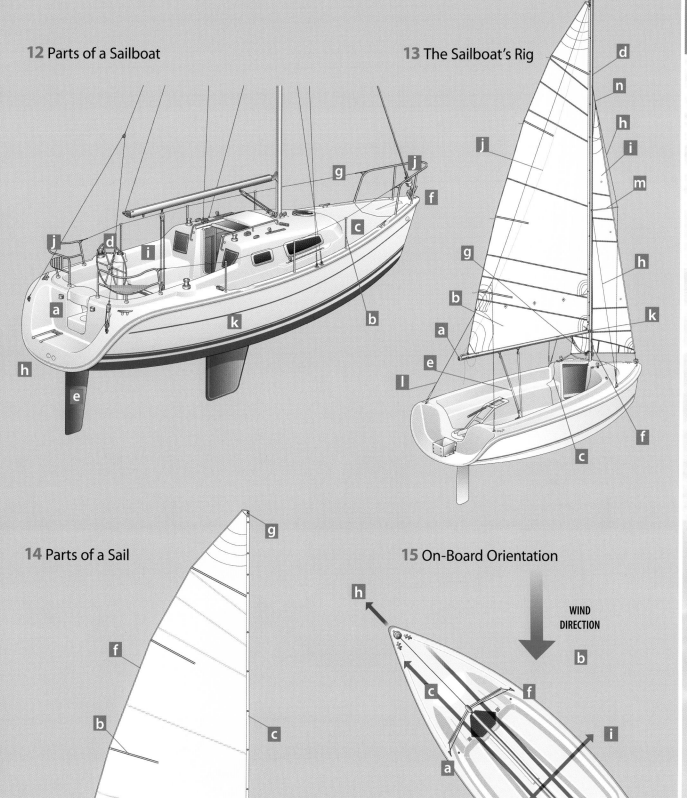

CHAPTER 2

Welcome aboard

People learn to sail in a variety of ways. Some grow up in sailing families, others absorb their knowledge by sailing with friends. Many take sailing courses, whether as youngsters in a youth sailing program or as adults at a sailing school. Whatever path they have taken, it's just part of the journey, because there is always more to learn about in this diverse and fascinating sport.

You can begin to learn about sailing on shore, by simply reading magazines and books, but ultimately you need to spend time on the water, and in this chapter we set sail. Remember, your first steps out on the water will be greatly enhanced under the tutelage of a qualified sailing instructor. Let's go sailing!

BOARDING

Before going sailing, you have to first get aboard the boat. On the face of it, boarding a sailboat might appear as easy as getting on a bus, but a misstep has led to many a sailor ending up in the water. Embarrassment might be the least of your problems when you consider the very real possibility of hitting your head or sustaining some other injury on the way to a sudden, unplanned swim.

EASY DOES IT

The essential difference is that the bus will remain stationary while the boat, even though it might be tied to the dock, will move in response to your movements when boarding.

Every boat and docking arrangement is slightly different. Sometimes you'll have to climb up to get aboard, sometimes down. Smaller and lighter boats pose a bigger challenge to boarding because they "feel" your movements more than bigger boats. So before boarding, ensure the boat is as close to the dock as possible. To do so, you may have to snug up on some *dock lines* (with which it's secured to the dock) and maybe ease off others.

In general the best place to board any boat is in the middle, near its widest point. Often, the shrouds offer a secure handhold. If your boat has lifelines, there may be a gate that you can simply open and walk through. Avoid boarding at the bow, where deck space is limited and the bow pulpit often presents an obstacle.

Before or during your big first step aboard, don't lean or push away on the boat. If the dock lines are slack, the boat will move away from the dock, leaving you suspended over the water — or even worse.

Because the deck might be wet and slippery, transfer your weight to the boat by stepping directly down onto the boat, rather than taking such a big step that your foot is pushing out at an angle. Think of what happens on ice. If you want to avoid slipping, you apply your weight directly downwards. Take the same precaution on a slippery sailboat deck.

To climb aboard a keelboat with lifelines:
① Take a firm grip on the shroud with one hand.
② Step up to the outer edge of the deck, one foot at a time.
③ When both feet are on the edge, wait for the boat to settle down — your movements may make it rock a little.
④ While still holding the shroud, step over the lifeline.

TIP *It's a matter of courtesy and tradition that before boarding someone else's boat, even when invited, you ask for "permission to come aboard."*

TIP *The "non-skid" soft-rubber soles of boat shoes cut through water and help grip the deck. Think of a pair of deck shoes as part of your personal safety gear — but remember, a wet deck can be slippery even with the best shoes. Going barefoot on a wet deck is risky because of the possibility of slipping and bashing your toes.*

TREAT SMALLER BOATS WITH GREAT RESPECT

Never board any boat with anything in your hand — you may be faced with the choice between dropping it and getting wet. Before boarding, hand your gear to someone or place it on the deck (as far from the edge as possible) and retrieve it after you have safely boarded.

TIP *Take special care when boarding a dinghy or smaller keelboat because of their limited stability. If you were to follow the instructions above and step on the edge of a small sailboat at its widest point, it would tip radically under your weight and you might soon be swimming! Aim to get your weight low and as close to the centerline of the boat as possible.*

TIP *To get off the boat, simply reverse the process, holding a shroud and taking your time and care with that big step down to the dock (or up if exiting a dinghy).*

The larger the boat, the bigger the step. Climbing aboard always requires care and sometimes requires agility.

The weight of a person stepping aboard can cause a smaller boat to tilt, which might be disconcerting if unexpected.

IN THE COCKPIT — THE BOAT'S CONTROLS

Once aboard, take a look around the cockpit and get familiar with its layout. This is the boat's contol center and you will need to know what the various controls are, where they are located, and how they function. The driving force of our sailboat is the wind flowing over the sails, and you control that by using the sheets to adjust the angle of the sails to the wind. You will steer the boat with the tiller or, on a bigger boat, the wheel.

TAKING THE HELM
— STEERING A SAILBOAT

Take hold of the tiller and push it back and forth. With the boat stationary, it will have no effect, because the rudder to which it's connected only generates a turning force when water is flowing over it. Under way, when you push the tiller to the left, the boat will turn to the right — opposite to the direction you move your hand. Push the tiller to the right and the boat will turn to the left. It's different, but after a little practice, steering with a tiller will become instinctive.

A steering wheel works the same way on a boat as in a car.

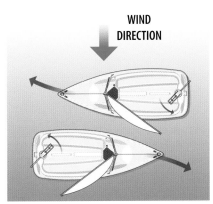

WIND DIRECTION

The boat turns in the opposite direction to that in which the tiller is pushed. Push it toward the sail to turn toward the wind, away from the sail to turn away from the wind.

THE MAINSHEET

Your primary means of trimming the mainsail, or adjusting its angle relative to the boat and to the wind, is the mainsheet. Imagine the wind blowing onto the port side of the boat. The mainsail and its attached boom will be pushed to the starboard side. The mainsheet controls how far the boom can travel. If the mainsheet is released,

the boom will go farther out and the sail will simply flap, aligned directly with the wind. When you pull in on the mainsheet, the boom will come in and the sail will begin to fill with wind and begin to drive the boat forward.

Right now, the mainsheet is hauled in tight to hold the boom steady (the boom topping lift is holding the boom up). When the time comes to hoist the mainsail, you will let the mainsheet run free to prevent the sail from catching the wind and making it difficult to raise. To get moving, you will want to make the mainsail fill with wind. You will do that by adjusting the mainsheet and by steering.

THE JIBSHEETS

The jib is controlled by two sheets, one on each side of the boat. If the wind is blowing on the port side of the boat, you will use the starboard jibsheet to adjust the trim of the jib, and vice versa. If the jib is not yet rigged, the sheets may not be in place.

The helmsman usually also controls the mainsheet, so he can adjust it at the same time as he changes course. On this boat, the mainsail's trim can be fine tuned with the traveler (inset).

PREPARING TO GO SAILING

Now that you know your way around the cockpit, we can begin to rig the sails and their control ropes — or lines, as you are learning to call them. Keep in mind that boats are rigged in a great variety of ways. Bigger cruising-oriented keelboats have their mainsail and jib stored in position ready to go, with the mainsail hooked up and under a cover on the boom and the jib rolled up on a roller-furling forestay. We will keep our instruction here focused on our small keelboat, where the sails will need to be fully rigged before sailing. It's a good thing to know how to do this no matter how your boat is set up. We start with the mainsail.

RIGGING THE MAINSAIL

After removing the mainsail from its bag, locate the tack. It will be at the forward end of the sail's foot. It has a distinctive 90 degree angle (the clew and head corners have smaller angles), and is also usually identifiable by the sailmaker's label attached nearby. The mainsail tack attaches to or near the gooseneck, at the forward end of the boom. The attachment is often by means of a shackle or pin through a ring or *grommet* in the sail.

At the other end of the sail's foot is the clew, which will be similarly fitted with a strong attachment point in the form of a grommet or ring.

There are three common methods for rigging the foot of the mainsail. In the simplest, the sail is attached to the boom only at the tack and the clew. The sail is then said to be a *loose footed* mainsail.

In the other two methods, the foot is attached also along the length of the boom, either by means of evenly spaced

slugs or with a *bolt rope*, a thick rope edge sewn onto the foot that slides into a groove along the top of the boom. With these arrangements, feed the slug or bolt rope end closest to the clew into the slot at the front of the boom and pull the clew all the way aft while continuing to feed the foot into the boom. When the foot is fully stretched, attach the clew by the means provided — usually a shackle.

The clew usually attaches to a car that can slide on a short track on the boom. The car's position can be adjusted by the *outhaul* to increase or reduce the tension in the sail's foot.

When the clew is secure, go forward and attach the tack at the gooseneck.

Next, insert the battens into the batten pockets, which have their openings at the leech. Take time to ensure that you are inserting the battens correctly. Often, they are all different lengths and each will fit perfectly in only one pocket. If one end is more flexible, insert that end first. Make sure the battens are secure as they

will be subjected to some very vigorous shaking when the sail flaps. A wide variety of systems is used to keep the battens in place including string ties and hook-and-loop fasteners like Velcro.

Now, locate the top corner of the sail, the head, and identify the system by which the luff will be attached to the mast. Often, this will be in a similar manner to the foot, with a bolt rope or slugs along the luff that slide into a track or slot running up the aft face of the mast.

A sail with a bolt-rope luff detaches completely from the mast as it's lowered and can't be pre-rigged, although you can feed the first foot or two into the slot and hold it up with the halyard.

If the system employs slugs, you may be able to feed most or all of them into the mast prior to hoisting. With this and similar systems, the luff remains attached securely to the mast after the sail is lowered, which makes things easier in strong winds and on bigger boats with the bigger sails.

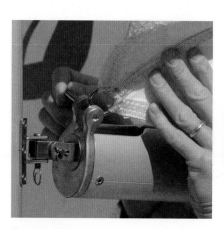

This mainsail has a ring sewn into its tack. A threaded pin secures it to a fitting on the forward end of the boom.

Battens support the leech of the mainsail. They slide into batten pockets that have their openings in the leech.

On some mainsails, slugs attached to the sail's luff slide in a groove in the aft face of the mast.

ATTACHING THE MAIN HALYARD

While we're working with the mainsail, we'll also attach the halyard, even though we'll have a few more things to do before hoisting the sail.

If you look *aloft*, toward the top of the mast, you'll see the halyard where it exits the aft side. Trace it down to the deck, where you'll find it shackled to a convenient piece of hardware. The other end of the halyard runs down the mast (often inside it, exiting through a hole or block at or near deck level) and ultimately is secured, or *made fast*, either on the mast or on deck, to a *cleat*, a fitting which can hold a line by means of friction (cleats and their use are covered in detail on pages 65 and 67). When you pull or jiggle the halyard near the cleat and see movement on the shackle end, you know you have correctly identified both ends of the same halyard (some boats have several halyards).

Unclip the shackle from its storage place. You may have to slack the halyard to do so, but be careful never to let go of either end.

You will notice that the top of the mainsail where you attach the halyard may be reinforced with a *headboard* of

metal or extra fabric. Look aloft to ensure the halyard isn't tangled or twisted up the mast and attach it securely to the head of the mainsail.

TIP *Never unfasten either end of any halyard and let it go. Always hold on to it or secure it temporarily. An accidental tug on the opposite end of an unsecured halyard can buy you, or someone else, a trip up the mast to retrieve it!*

As there is some more rigging to do, we'll wait to hoist the mainsail until departure is imminent. Sails left hoisted while the boat sits at the dock can cause problems — a sudden windshift could fill the sails and blow the boat into some hard object (like another boat or the dock). Whenever possible, sails shouldn't be allowed to flap because it wears them out. Once you have the mainsail foot, luff (if you're using the slug system), and halyard attached, you can fold and secure it on the boom exactly the way it's done in "Stowing the Mainsail" (see page 86). To keep the halyard from swinging about, tie the head of the sail down with a *sail tie* (a short length of cloth webbing or rope used to keep sails tidy), or hook the

Somebody let go of the halyard! Fortunately, an agile volunteer was on hand to climb the mast and retrieve it.

halyard under a cleat on the mast, snug the halyard, and make it fast on its cleat.

With practice, you and your crew may work on several tasks simultaneously and you'll be ready to hoist right away but, for now, we'll assume that you have to help with all aspects of preparing the boat. Right now, it's time to move forward and rig the jib.

The head of this mainsail is reinforced with a headboard. The halyard attaches to it by means of a special shackle.

Once the foot of the mainsail has been attached to the boom and the luff slides inserted into the slot in the mast, the sail can be loosely flaked and secured to the boom with a sail tie. It is now ready to be hoisted when it's time to go sailing.

RIGGING THE JIB

Some sailing instructors like to take their students out on their first sail under mainsail only, to keep the focus on steering and the trim of only one sail. Virtually every modern keelboat sails perfectly well under mainsail alone (sailing with only the jib can be quite a bit more tricky). And some maneuvers, such as docking under sail, are commonly performed with just the mainsail up. But when sailing in open water, looking for best performance and handling, the jib is an integral part of your sailboat's power plant. Plus it gives more for the crew to do!

JIB ATTACHMENT SYSTEMS

As with the mainsail, several systems can be employed for rigging the jib depending on the size and performance level of the boat. On our small keelboat, the two most common ways for attaching the jib to the forestay are with either *hanks* or a *luff tape*.

In the latter system, a tape that includes a thin bolt rope is sewn along the jib's luff. The tape slides into and is hoisted up a groove in a special forestay device called a *headfoil*. This system often includes a roller furler which allows the jib to be stored in a tight roll wrapped around the forestay/headfoil.

Hanks are small fittings or cloth tabs with snaps that are permanently affixed at equal intervals along the jib's luff. This method of attachment has an advantage

in that the entire luff of the sail can be connected to the forestay while the jib is still on deck and remains so after it's dropped, making it more manageable, especially in rough conditions.

Since a jib on a roller-furler system would be already rigged and hoisted, we'll focus here on attaching a jib with hanks on its luff.

① Remove the jib from its bag, lay it out on the foredeck, and identify its three corners. The head is the narrowest. At the bottom of the luff, distinguished by its hanks, is the tack, where you'll usually find the sailmaker's label. Orient the sail so that the tack is nearest the bow and the clew is aft, closest to the mast.

② Secure the tack of the jib to the fitting at the base of the forestay using the shackle or other device provided.

③ Beginning with the hank nearest the tack, attach the hanks to the forestay. By working carefully from tack to head, you will avoid a common and embarrassing mistake — clipping one or more hanks on upside down so that when the sail is hoisted it has a twist in the luff.

TIP *Never stand on sailcloth that's been spread out on the deck. It's very slick, and you could easily lose your balance.*

④ If the two jibsheets (the lines you will use to trim the sail) are not already attached, tie one end of each to the clew ring or grommet. The preferred knot is the bowline (which you'll find with other useful knots on page 64).

TIP *When rigging a jib with a luff tape, you have to wait until the sail is ready to hoist before sliding the top of the luff tape (near the head) into the opening ramp in the headfoil's groove.*

⑤ Find the jib halyard shackle by looking up the mast for a halyard that exits on the forward side near the forestay's attachment point. Trace the halyard downward to find where the shackle is secured, then tug on it to locate the other end, which will likely be secured on the mast. Detach the jib halyard shackle from its stowed location and attach it immediately to the head of the jib. Look up to ensure that the halyard is clear and not snagged or wrapped anywhere. Make sure the halyard is still cleated at the other end.

This jib has a luff tape that slides into a headfoil. A feeder at the base of the headfoil guides the tape into its groove, but it needs a helping hand to get it started.

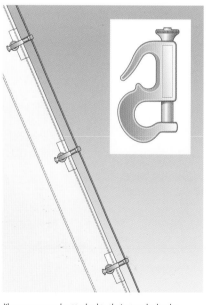

Jibs are commonly attached to their stays by hanks. Shown here is a piston hank. It's opened by pulling on the button against an internal spring that holds it closed.

When preparing to rig the jib, a crewmember checks that she has hold of both ends of the same halyard and that it is not fouled or tangled aloft.

....

TIP *If the halyard shackle has a screw pin, use a tool such as a shackle key or pliers to give it more than just a hand tightening.*

....

⑥ Unless you are going to hoist the jib immediately, flake the rest of the sail to keep it compact and low and secure it to the boat with one or more sail ties.

⑦ Lead the jibsheets from the clew back into the cockpit, one on either side of the mast. Every boat will have a slightly different system for running the jibsheets. If it's not obvious, it's considered good etiquette to ask someone how they should be led. Each sheet will usually pass through a block or other device near the deck and, perhaps through another *fairlead* so it leads *fair* (unobstructed and at the correct angle) to its cleat or winch. When you've led the jibsheet back to the cockpit through the correct path of blocks and fairleads, tie a figure-eight stopper knot (see page 65) in its end so it can't be pulled back through accidentally.

ROLLER-FURLING JIB

Roller furling for jibs has been around for decades. Modern designs are reliable enough that it has become standard

Jibsheets lead from the clew of the jib, through blocks, and aft to the cockpit. Details vary from boat to boat.

equipment on a great variety of sailboats. It works in a similar manner to a roll-up window blind: The sail essentially rolls up along its own luff.

On small boats, the luff of the sail itself might be stiffened by a wire or high-strength rope. On bigger boats, the luff is held in a headfoil that can rotate around a forestay or headstay (see opposite page).

The tack of the roller-furling jib attaches to the top of the furling drum around which the furling line is wound. The head attaches to a swivel which is hauled aloft with the halyard.

Once it has been hoisted, a roller-furling jib usually stays hoisted for the season. The furling line is led aft to the cockpit. When you're sailing and want to

To unfurl a roller-furling jib, the crew pulls on the jibsheet, at right. As the sail unwinds, the furling line winds up on the roller-furling drum, above. Reversing the procedure — pulling the furling line while easing the sheet — furls the sail.

HANKED-ON JIB

Flaking a hanked-on jib is very easy.
1. Pull the luff so that it snakes from hank to hank on alternating sides of the forestay.
2. Push the hanks down so the folds of the sail lie tightly together.
3. Trace the folds to the leech and foot and pull back on the sail to make them even and tidy .
4. Hold the flaked sail together with a sail tie.
5. Tie the sail to a convenient item of hardware on the deck.

set the jib, all you have to do is ease the furling line while you pull on the jibsheet (see page 45). To furl the sail, you ease the sheet and pull on the furling line, which turns the drum which rolls up the sail.

When the sail is furled, the furling line must be firmly cleated so the sail cannot accidentally unfurl.

USING WINCHES — ADD POWER TO YOUR ELBOW

Everything is ready for us to take the boat out sailing, but before we set sail, you need to learn how to do a bit of grinding — on a winch. On dinghies, you can handle the loads created by the sails without the need for much mechanical assistance, but on keelboats, the loads increase and even the strongest person needs help. A winch provides both the mechanical advantage to pull on a highly loaded line and a means of holding that line in place. Our small keelboat will likely be equipped with manually operated single- or two-speed winches.

LOADING A WINCH

To use a winch you must first wrap the line in question around it — before the line comes under load. All winches rotate only in one direction. Most winches made today turn clockwise, but to ensure you don't wrap the line backwards (a mistake everyone makes at first), spin the winch with your hand to check which way it rotates. Add your wraps in the direction of rotation, so that when you pull on the line, it turns the winch drum.

Simply wrapping a line once or twice around a winch will not make it easier to pull by hand alone, but the friction between the line and the drum helps you hold, or *snub*, the line against the load on it (the winch drum cannot rotate backwards). The more wraps, the greater the friction, and you can hold a line that is under tremendous load.

Make your first wrap around the bottom of the winch and work upward with your subsequent wraps. How many wraps? Well, that depends. Before the load comes on, start with the minimum — one to three depending on the situation. Too many wraps make it harder to pull and you risk a bad tangle (see "override" page 37), but be ready to add more wraps as the load comes on.

OPERATING THE WINCH — PULLING AND EASING

Once the load on the line has built to the point where you can no longer pull it by hand, use the winch handle. It fits into the socket on top of the winch (and it may have a locking device operated by your thumb).

Before you insert the handle add another wrap or two to give you a better grip on the line. Hold the *tail*, the end of the line that's coming off the winch, taut with two hands and, holding the tail below the top of the winch, pass it around the drum. Don't let either hand get any closer than about one foot from the winch. Be careful, adding or removing wraps under high load can be dangerous if not done correctly.

Only insert the handle when you need it for grinding. When you are pulling the line by hand, you want the top of the winch clear so you can swiftly add wraps before the load builds.

Grinding (turning the winch with the handle) greatly increases your pulling power because of the lever arm of the handle and the winch's gears. When grinding, keep steady tension on the tail, to prevent it from slipping. If the line begins to slip on the winch, either pull

harder on the line or add another wrap.

To operate a single-speed winch, you turn the handle in the direction of rotation of the drum: clockwise. The handle may ratchet in the opposite direction, which is helpful when using it one-handed.

Two-speed winches have a second set of gears to give even more purchase for handling the high loads encountered in strong winds or on larger boats. This second gear is engaged by turning the handle counter-clockwise; however, the winch drum still rotates clockwise.

Under high load, a winch is most effective when one crewmember grinds while another *tails* by pulling on the tail of the line as it comes off the winch. The person grinding should move into as steady and comfortable a position over the top of the winch as possible, shoulders facing the winch, and grind in full circles for maximum speed and power.

One person can do both jobs, albeit a little more slowly, by tailing with one hand while grinding with the other. Remember that when working with one arm you can pull harder on the handle than you can push, so use the ratchet on the winch to your advantage.

When pulling a line that's coming from a winch, work hand over hand to maintain tension.

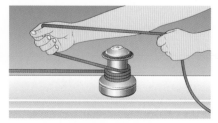

To add a wrap, keep tension in the line and pass it around the winch while keeping your hands away from the drum.

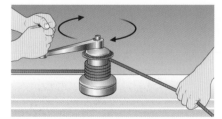

To use the winch's power, insert the handle and use it to turn the drum while someone else tails the line.

SAFETY TIP *Take care that your fingers never get between the line and the winch. Work deliberately and, when tailing, keep your hands as far from the winch as practicable — about two feet is good.*

As you grind, make sure you, or someone who is guiding you, can clearly see the sail or whatever is being affected by your grinding — you can create enough force to cause damage if something is amiss.

After you've finished grinding and have the line, which might be a halyard or a sheet, set correctly, ensure the tail is well secured on a cleat with a *cleat hitch* (see page 65 for how to tie it) or in its *jammer* (see page 67), a mechanical device for holding a loaded line.

SAFETY TIP *To avoid possible injuries, always remove the winch handle from the winch after cleating the line. Secure the handle in its proper stowage location — winch handles don't float!*

EASING AND UNLOADING

At some point, the line you have tensioned with the winch will have to be *eased*, or let out. Before uncleating a line prior to easing it, first make sure the tail is clear. Then, remembering there's a lot of load on that line and you're going to be holding it, ensure you can keep sufficient tension on the tail of the line coming from the winch.

Before you take it off the cleat, take hold of the tail between the winch and the cleat so you can maintain tension on the wraps on the winch.

TIP *If you encounter undue resistance when using a winch, stop grinding and look for a reason. If the line or the sail it's attached to has fouled, winding harder will lead to a breakage.*

Once you've uncleated the tail, hold it at the level of the winch and begin to ease the line by carefully relaxing the force with which you're holding it. This should allow the line to slip on the winch drum while you control the pace at which it pays out. If you will be releasing the line completely, as the load on the line decreases, you can begin to take wraps off the winch to facilitate its release.

SAFETY TIP *Before easing any line, make sure that its tail cannot become entangled with anything as it runs out — that goes especially for body parts, your own or anyone else's.*

SAFETY TIP *Think first! A highly loaded line can burn your hands or worse if it releases quickly when you are holding it. Don't sail with finger rings — they can get caught on a line. If you are wearing sailing gloves, make sure they fit snugly because the extra fabric can get caught up in a winch.*

WINCH BUMMERS — THE OVERRIDE

Occasionally, even experienced sailors can get an *override*, when the tail of the line becomes pinched under the wraps on the winch drum, immobilizing the winch. An override can be very difficult to untangle and, depending on the circumstances, may be a serious problem.

If the override is on the jibsheet winch, for example, you might have to rig a temporary second jibsheet with which to take the load off the stuck sheet. Or you might turn the boat, downwind or upwind, to unload the jibsheet.

A common cause of an override is having too many wraps on the winch drum when you are rapidly taking up the slack on an unloaded line.

SELF-TAILING WINCH

A self-tailing winch is fitted with a clever device on its top that tails in the line as you grind and at the same time secures it, taking the place of a jammer or cleat.

Using the self-tailer adds friction, so we don't use it when pulling in a lot of line by hand. As the load increases to where pulling by hand is difficult, first add those extra needed wraps on the winch in the usual way. After the last wrap, pass the tail over the stripping arm, which feeds it into the set of jaws at the top of the winch that grip the line tightly without damaging it. You now have both hands free to apply to the winch handle.

The best use of the self tailer is in making adjustments to a highly loaded line.

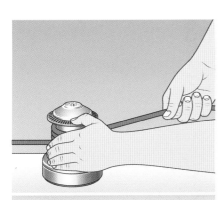

When easing the line, you can (carefully!) use the palm of your hand to adjust the friction between line and drum.

An override occurs when the line leading onto the winch gets on top of the wraps already on the winch.

LET'S GO SAILING — HOISTING SAILS AND CASTING OFF

Okay, we're getting close to the best part — your first sail! The sails are rigged and you're checked out on working the winches — the wide blue awaits. Are we ready to go sailing yet? Is all the crew aboard? Do you have the proper clothing and sunscreen on? (see page 112) Is all loose gear stowed securely? Are your cell phone and wallet stored in a dry spot? If so, it's time for a few words from the skipper.

SKIPPER'S PRE-SAIL BRIEFING

Before you cast off to go sailing, the skipper will want to advise everyone aboard about what to expect and also address a few safety topics. Every skipper is different. For now, your instructor will be giving the briefing and it will reflect his experience and his methods for running his ship. He will include instructions on where to find and operate the boat's safety equipment. He will also instruct the crew on how to conduct themselves so as to ensure a safe and enjoyable experience for all.

The briefing will end with a short checklist: Are the sails attached properly? Are the jibsheets tied to the sail and led aft properly? Is the mainsheet rigged and ready? Is the boom vang free to run? Are the rudder and tiller (or wheel) in position and ready to be operated? Have you ascertained the wind direction? If the answers to all these questions are "yes" then you're ready to set sail.

(see page 112)

THINKING OF YOUR SAFETY - DANGER AREAS

In Chapter 5, we'll cover safety in greater depth, but all sailors should be aware of the areas on a sailboat that are potentially dangerous. Sometimes your role on board may have you performing a necessary job at one of these places. That's okay, just be extra careful, and pay attention to what the boat is doing!

■ Anywhere in or above the plane of the boom. In certain maneuvers, the boom will swing across the cockpit, sometimes with a lot of force. Keep your head down and also stay out of the path of the boom vang and mainsheet, as they will follow it.

■ On the leeward (downwind) side of the boat, especially if the boat is heeling.

■ In the way of the jib and jibsheets during a maneuver. The sail and its sheets are like whips when the sail flaps.

■ Anywhere outside of the cockpit, especially when you are walking or standing.

■ At the bow and stern — hang on! The boat's motion is accentuated here.

■ Near any open hatches or slippery areas on deck such as varnished wood or plastic hatch covers. Walking on a sail is like walking on ice!

Get the idea? — normally the windward side of the cockpit below the level of the boom is safest.

Before giving the order to cast off, it's customary for the skipper to give the crew some pointers about the boat's equipment. He will also offer tips on how to have fun while sailing safely.

MAINSAIL FIRST

On our small keelboat, we'll be hoisting the mainsail first and getting under way and out into open water before hoisting the jib. This is fairly typical, because having only one sail to deal with keeps things simple when getting out of tight quarters.

HOISTING THE MAINSAIL

When hoisting the mainsail, it is essential that the boat be oriented *head to wind*, that is, with the bow pointed directly at the oncoming wind. This will allow the luff to slide up the mast freely with minimal friction and will also prevent the mainsail from filling with wind while you are hoisting it (which puts so much load on the halyard that you might not be able to hoist it). In a pinch, and depending on how the mainsail is rigged, you can be within about 20 degrees of head to wind.

If the boat is at a dock, you may have to move it into a position where it's pointing into the wind. If the orientation of your dock area allows, secure the boat with a single dock line running from the bow to the leeward side of the dock, so it will naturally point into the wind.

Next, prepare the crew for their roles in the action. One or two may have to go forward to help with the hoist. A small sailboat is a surprisingly lively platform, so any time you must leave the cockpit, find a secure position from which to work. Sometimes that means using the shrouds or mast for support. Bravado and dignity take a back seat to safety and staying on the boat.

SAFETY TIP *Whenever you leave the cockpit, keep your weight low by bending your knees. Use one hand to hold on at all times. Heed the old sailors' saying, "One hand for the ship and one hand for yourself."*

Once everybody is in position, you are ready to raise the mainsail. On our small keelboat, that proceeds with the following sequence of steps:

① Remove the sail ties (but don't let the sail fall into the water!).

② If the aft end of the boom is not supported by a topping lift but is tied off by a line from the backstay, free it and lower the boom end to the deck.

③ Look aloft and ensure the halyard is clear and hasn't fouled on anything.

④ Haul in on the tail of the halyard to take out excess slack.

⑤ The boom has to be free to rise, so double check that anything that holds it down — mainsheet, boom vang, and Cunningham or downhaul — are uncleated and free to run.

⑥ Announce to the crew that you are hoisting the main. This is both a call to stations for the crew and also a warning for them to get clear of the boom, which will swing about in an arc over the center of the cockpit. If your mainsail has a bolt-rope luff, one crew will need to move forward and feed it into the entrance slot in the mast as the sail is hoisted.

⑦ Hoist the halyard by hand (if it's around a winch, with one or two wraps) until it gets too difficult. (If the luff rope jams where it feeds into the mast, ease the halyard enough so the person feeding the luff can clear the jam.) Use the winch handle to complete the hoist and then cleat the halyard.

TIP *Often the halyard is so rigged that a crew standing at the side of the mast will have an ideal position to apply hoisting power — this is called jumping the halyard.*

⑧ Ease the boom topping lift enough that it will not become taut when the mainsheet is pulled tight.

⑨ Coil the tail of the halyard, wrap it, and stow it properly (see page 68). Adjust the outhaul, Cunningham, and boom vang as needed and cleat them.

TIP *If you don't have a winch, you can increase your pulling power on any taut line, such as a halyard, by* swigging *or swaying it. Take a turn under a cleat with the tail, pull the line away at a 90 degree angle like a bow string, and then quickly take up on the tail. This is a great two-person technique and works really well for a person jumping the halyard at the mast.*

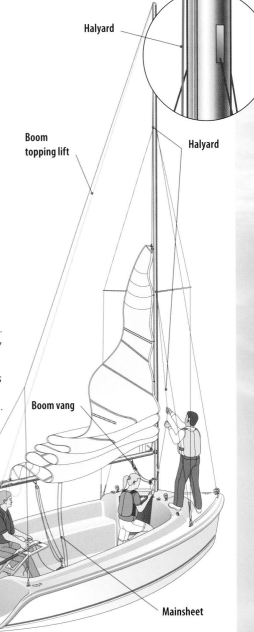

Halyard

Boom topping lift

Halyard

Boom vang

Mainsheet

GETTING THE BOAT MOVING AND KEEPING IT MOVING

The mainsail is up and fluttering, you have the mainsheet ready for trimming it, and you know how to use the tiller for steering. It's time to cast off and feel the boat moving and see how it responds when you work the sheet and the tiller. Leaving and returning to the dock are often the most challenging parts of the day because of the confined space and the need to sail at low speeds — when the rudder doesn't "work" as well. Your instructor may choose to drive the boat out into open water before handing you the helm for your first sail.

SAILING OFF THE DOCK

How you go about leaving the dock is dictated by the wind direction. If it's blowing away from the dock, the procedure is simple.

....

TIP *Ever since you raised the mainsail, the mainsheet has been slack, allowing the sail to flutter, or luff. (As you learn the lingo of sailing you'll find several words have multiple meanings. Luff is one of them.) Now that you are ready to leave the dock, station one crew at the mainsheet and another at the tiller (or on a small boat, one person can do both jobs). The goal is to get the boat turned away from the wind, out of the no-sail zone, and onto a reach before trimming the mainsail.*

....

Here's one way to sail free of the dock when the wind is blowing off the dock.
① Double the bow line, so it leads from the boat, around the dock fitting and back to the boat. When you're ready, you can then cast off one end from the boat and pull it aboard from the other. Cast off the other dock lines and let the boat swing to the bow line.
② Cast off the bow line and let the wind blow the boat off the dock. Hold the tiller all the way over to one side so it's pointing in the direction you want the bow to turn to rotate the boat away from the wind. Keep the mainsheet fully released.

....

TIP *Remember, with the boat going backwards, the tiller works backwards — the bow will turn in the direction the tiller is pointing instead of away from it.*

③ Once you have turned so the wind is on the beam, slowly pull in on the mainsheet so the sail begins to fill. Move the tiller back to the center.
④ As the sail fills and the boat begins to move forward, pull the tiller slightly to windward so the boat will turn farther away from the wind and pick up speed. This will increase the flow of water over the rudder and give more steering control.
⑤ When the boat is pointing toward

clear water, adjust the tiller to steer the boat in a straight line … you're sailing!

....

TIP *The hardest part of this maneuver is getting the boat rotated and pointed onto a reach so that the sail will "work". If there is sufficient space, a crew on the dock can pull the boat with the bow line to get it moving forward and then give one good push on the shrouds before stepping aboard.*

....

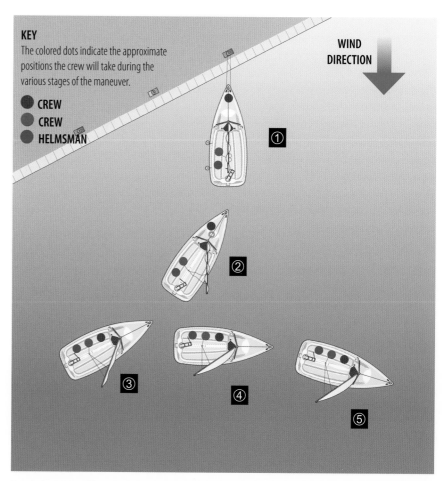

KEY
The colored dots indicate the approximate positions the crew will take during the various stages of the maneuver.
● CREW
● CREW
● HELMSMAN

WIND DIRECTION

① ② ③ ④ ⑤

Once the boat is untied from the dock, the wind will blow it backwards. It will also tend to blow the bow to one side. Use the tiller to help it push you in the desired direction. The tiller will work "backwards" until the boat starts moving forward.

From some berths, the path to open water is something of an obstacle course and best negotiated under mainsail only.

If the wind is blowing the boat toward the dock, any sort of sailing departure is not going to be pretty and may be impossible. Does your boat have an engine? Whenever possible, make your life easy and move the boat so it hangs downwind from the dock before hoisting sail and departing.

LEAVING THE DOCK UNDER POWER

If the boat has an engine and the area immediately around the dock is quite constrained, it might be prudent to leave the dock under power alone. Once the boat's in open water, it will be easy for the helmsman to hold the boat pointed into the wind while powering very slowly forward. The process of hoisting the main remains the same as above.

(Look for opportunities, though, to practice sailing off the dock. It's pretty satisfying — and never fails to impress bystanders — when you carry it off without a hitch.)

SAILING AT LAST

For the first few minutes, everything will feel a little alien. Enjoy the sensation while you concentrate on steering a straight course toward open water where you have room to hoist the jib.

You'll notice that when you're trying to steer straight, the boat will often "pull" to one side — like a car with a soft front tire. The amount of "pull" will change with wind speed and the point of sail. That's because the force of the wind on the sail is both driving the boat forward and making it want to turn — usually toward the wind. You'll "feel" all these forces on the boat, sails, and rudder as pressure transmitted through the tiller. Feeling is a big part of sailing, and with time on the boat your sensitivity will increase. You'll learn to use the feel of the helm to sense when you need to make adjustments to the sails.

....

TIP *When steering with a tiller or a wheel, sit on the windward side of the cockpit for the best view of the sails and the boat's surroundings. Sitting just forward of the end of the tiller gives you the best leverage and a tiller extension, or hiking stick, lets you sit farther outboard for an even better view of the sails and the water ahead.*

....

STEER A STEADY COURSE

Amid all the new sensations and distractions of being on a boat, on the water, and under the influence of wind and wave, steering a straight and steady

course can be illusive. At the same time as you push and pull on the tiller, you will be watching the sails and looking around you for other boats and potential hazards. Simply looking at the water ahead doesn't help much because it too is in motion.

When you begin learning to sail, you won't be far from land. Whenever you sail toward the land you can pick a landmark (the farther away the better) to steer toward. If you are headed toward the sea, look for a cloud near the horizon to use as a reference.

To see how good a job you're doing, look at the wake the boat leaves in the water behind it. If it looks like a snake, you are working too hard: make small, gentle adjustments with the tiller and give the boat time to respond to them.

It does seem as though there's a lot to do just to get started, but pretty soon you'll have all the details down pat and getting under way will become a key part of building up anticipation for a great day on the water.

LEAVING A MOORING

When a boat is tied to a mooring buoy, it will naturally lie head to wind, especially with the mainsail raised and luffing, unless it's being affected by a strong current. Use the same technique as described above to get the boat out of the no-sail zone and sailing forward, but plan ahead so as to sail clear of other moored boats.

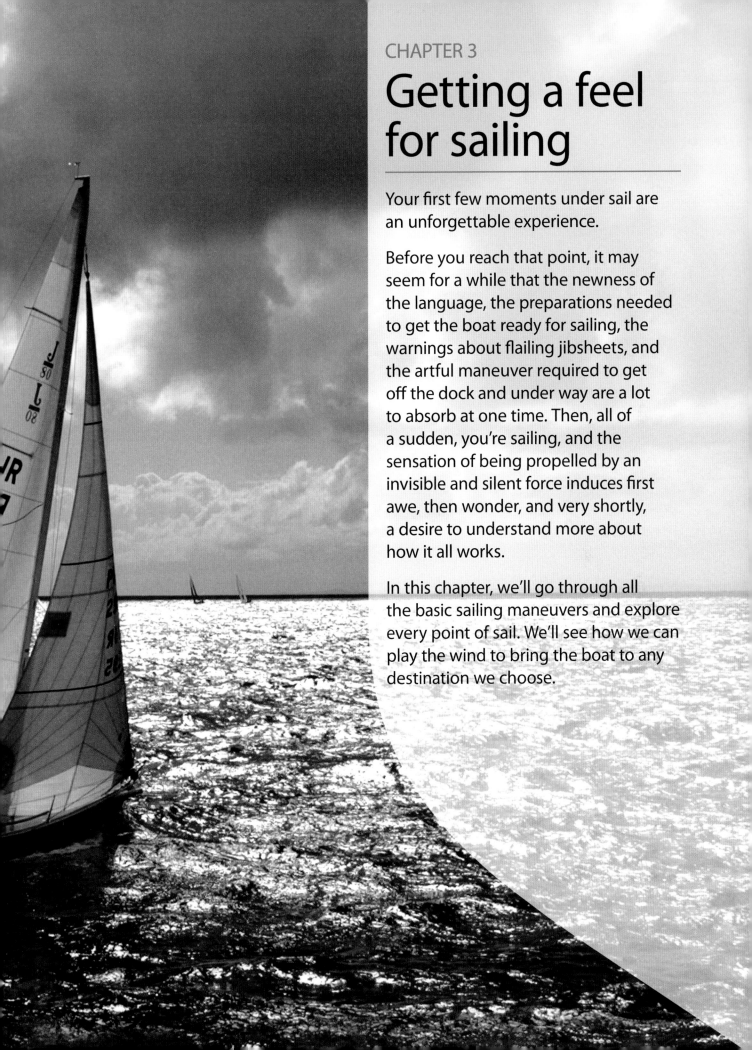

CHAPTER 3

Getting a feel for sailing

Your first few moments under sail are an unforgettable experience.

Before you reach that point, it may seem for a while that the newness of the language, the preparations needed to get the boat ready for sailing, the warnings about flailing jibsheets, and the artful maneuver required to get off the dock and under way are a lot to absorb at one time. Then, all of a sudden, you're sailing, and the sensation of being propelled by an invisible and silent force induces first awe, then wonder, and very shortly, a desire to understand more about how it all works.

In this chapter, we'll go through all the basic sailing maneuvers and explore every point of sail. We'll see how we can play the wind to bring the boat to any destination we choose.

IT'S ALL ABOUT TRIM

Now that you're clear of the dock and sailing in open water, you can begin to learn to optimize your course and sail trim. Start off by sailing along on a beam reach and experiment with making some small adjustments with the tiller to get a feel for how both the boat and the sail react. This is also a good time to learn a couple more sailors' terms that again relate to the wind. To *head up* is to turn the bow of the boat toward the wind, which you do by pushing the tiller to leeward, or if your boat has a wheel, turn it to windward; to *bear away* is to turn it away from the wind, which you do by pulling the tiller to windward or turning the wheel to leeward.

TRIM FOR COURSE

Although you might have hoisted the jib by now, we'll keep the focus here on steering and mainsail trim. However, the same rules will apply to jib trim. Proper sail trim is a function of both the boat's course and the wind direction. To keep things simple, steer straight on a beam reach with the mainsail full of wind and slowly ease the mainsheet until the sail begins to show a small "bubble", or luff, along its front edge (the "other" luff). If you keep easing the sheet, more and more of the sail will be luffing and your speed will rapidly drop as the sail loses effectiveness. Pull back in on the sheet slowly until the bubble at the luff just disappears. The sail is now properly trimmed and generating maximum lift.

If you trim in more, the sail will look nice and full with no luffing but it will lose power because it's over-trimmed. This highlights a very important point: A "full" sail is not necessarily properly trimmed. The only way to be sure is to ease the sheet (while still holding that steady course) until you see the tiny beginning of the luff on the leading edge of the mainsail. That's why the golden rule of sail trim is, "When in doubt — let it out!"

Now, with the sail properly trimmed for the beam reach, push the tiller slightly to leeward, so the boat begins to head up, and watch the luff of the sail. It will begin to luff again — because your course change altered the angle of the wind flow on the sail. Bear away, back to your previous course, and the sail will fill again.

> **TIP** *Two ways to stop a sail from luffing:*
> ① *Bear away*
> ② *Trim the sheet*

Head up a little, steady up on your new course, and trim the sail to the new point of sail.

If you continue to do this — steering closer to the wind and pulling in the mainsheet to keep the sail full — you will reach a point at which the sail is as tightly trimmed as you can get it, with the boom lying close to the boat's centerline, but the sail is still luffing. This indicates you are trying to sail too close to the wind and have entered the no-sail zone. Continue on this present heading and the boat will come to a stop.

GETTING INTO — AND OUT OF — IRONS

If the boat does come to a stop, with the sail fully luffing and the bow pointing into the wind, it is *in irons*. The sail is not working, and with no forward motion the tiller is useless. Every sailor has experienced this predicament and right now it's an opportunity to learn the crucial trick of getting out of irons and out of the no-sail zone. Your exit strategy is similar to how you got going off the dock or mooring — use the wind:

① Release the mainsheet so it's free to run and push the tiller all the way to one side or the other.
② As the boat begins to move backwards it will begin to turn. Keep the tiller jammed over until the boat is well out of the no-sail zone — with the wind on the beam.
③ Slowly trim the mainsail and bring the tiller toward the center and you're off again, on a beam reach.

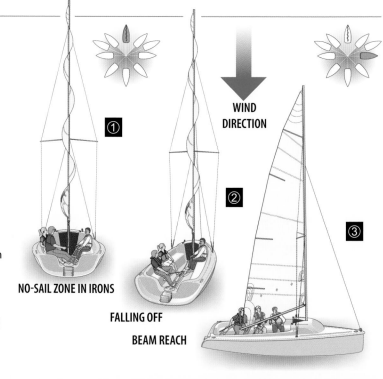

WIND DIRECTION

NO-SAIL ZONE IN IRONS

FALLING OFF

BEAM REACH

TIME FOR THE JIB

While the mainsail is usually the first sail to be hoisted, there is no set time to hoist the jib. Conditions permitting, there is absolutely nothing wrong with hoisting it at the dock or on the mooring. And while we could sail all day under mainsail alone, adding the jib will give us more speed and more things for our crew to do. The jib is much easier to raise than the mainsail because it can be hoisted quite easily on any point of sail, making it the go-to sail if you need sail power in a hurry. Here, we will be hoisting the jib under way.

RAISING THE JIB

While sailing on a broad reach, choose an open area and raise the jib as follows:

① If you lashed the jib or the halyard to the deck or lifelines, you'll have to leave the cockpit to untie it. Remember, one hand for the ship, one hand for yourself — the boat is moving now and you might be feeling some wave action. And watch out for that slippery sailcloth! If your jib has a luff-tape system, you will stay forward to help feed the luff into the groove in the headfoil as the sail is smoothly hoisted.

② If someone is going to "jump" the halyard at the mast, have that crewmember move safely forward.

③ Sight up the halyard from the jib to the top of the mast to make sure it can run free.

④ Trace the jibsheets from the clew to the cockpit and make sure they, too, are rigged correctly and free to run. Haul in any excess slack, and neatly coil or flake the tails in the cockpit.

⑤ Make sure the windward jibsheet is completely free. With the leeward jibsheet, take a couple of preparatory wraps around the winch, but don't put tension on the sheet until the sail has been hoisted.

⑥ Raise the jib, as you did the mainsail, by hauling on the halyard. If the boat has a headfoil, hoist steadily and not too fast for the crew feeding the luff tape.

⑦ Apply enough tension to the luff to remove any "scallops" in the luff between the hanks. Too much tension will create vertical wrinkles along the luff.

⑧ Cleat the halyard and neatly coil the line the way you did for the main halyard. Hang it on the mast or stow it in a secure yet accessible area.

⑨ Trim the leeward jibsheet until the sail stops luffing, then cleat it. If the windward-side sheet has wrapped itself around the leeward sheet, a light tug on the windward sheet should untangle them.

....

TIP *When sailing, the leeward jibsheet is often referred to as the* working sheet — *because it's, well, the one doing the work. The windward sheet is called the* lazy sheet.

....

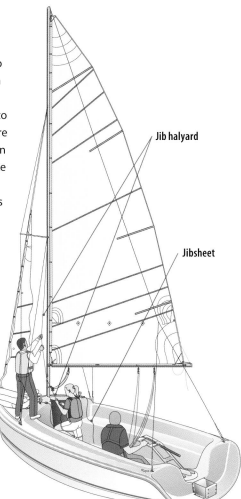

Jib halyard

Jibsheet

ROLLER-FURLING JIB

If you have a jib on a roller furler, steer the boat on a broad reach. Trace the jibsheets from the clew to the cockpit and make sure they are rigged correctly and their tails coiled or faked and ready for use. Then, find the furling line, which is wound on the spool at the base of the forestay and leads back to the cockpit. Make sure it's uncleated and ready to run free. When ready, start pulling in on the leeward jibsheet and the sail will begin to unroll. As the partially unfurled sail begins to fill, the wind will finish the job — just keep a little tension on the furling line so it winds up tidily on the spool. Trim the sail as in step 9 above and you're off!

....

TIP *Although raising or unfurling a jib is possible on any point of sail, a broad reach is nice because there is no heel and the motion of the boat is steadier for any crew operating at the mast and on the* foredeck, *the area of the deck forward of the mast. Also, the jib is blanketed* from the wind by the mainsail, making for an easier hoist.

....

Roller furling makes easy work of setting the jib: ease the furling line while pulling on the leeward jibsheet.

THE POWER OF TWO

Now that the jib is contributing you will notice a big difference in both the boat's maneuverability and its speed. Particularly when you sail closer to the wind, the two sails work together, so that the sum of their power is greater than the individual parts: The presence of the jib boosts the flow of air over the mainsail; the presence of the mainsail boosts the flow over the jib. All this adds up to more speed, which means more fun for the crew!

WORKING WITH TWO SAILS

The general rules of sail trim covered above — when in doubt, let it out — apply for the jib too, but because the two sails interact with each other and the wind, it takes more attention to keep them working together. Let's get some practice with our new combination while we explore some of the points of sail:
① Begin on a beam reach in open water with the mainsheet and jib trimmed correctly, both just on the verge of luffing.
② Ease the jibsheet about two feet very slowly and in control. The sail will begin to luff at the front edge. Now start pulling the sheet in — using the winch handle if needed — until the "bubbling"

at the sail's front edge just disappears. Just to see what happens, pull in the jibsheet another two feet. The jib will be over-trimmed, but the mainsail will now be luffing along its front edge — even though you haven't touched its sheet! The sails are out of balance and the wind flowing over the over-trimmed jib is blowing into the mainsail causing it to luff. When both sails are trimmed correctly, the wind accelerates through the slot between the leech of the jib and the luff of the main adding to both sails' aerodynamic power. Poor trim on either sail will disturb the airflow over both and slow the boat. The balance in the trim of both sails is

critical to their joint effectiveness, and the best sailors pay close attention to it.
③ Ease the jib until both sails are working together again.
④ Turn toward the wind slowly onto a close reach. As you head up, the sails will begin to luff. Trim both sails until both are correctly trimmed and enjoy the feel of the wind and heeling of the boat.

....
TIP *If you don't have enough crew to trim both sails at the same time, trim the jib first and then the mainsail. This will help you balance the sail trim more easily.*
....

On a beam reach, trim the sails so their luffs stay firm.

 BEAM REACH

⑤ Now slowly bear away, past a beam reach and onto a broad reach. As you turn away from the wind, the boat will level out and the wind will seem to get lighter. Cease your turn as soon as the jib begins to collapse inward (this happens because it's blanketed by the mainsail, indicating you are almost sailing on a run), and head back up just a few degrees toward the wind until the jib fills again. If you have not eased your mainsheet and jibsheet, both sails look full but are quite over-trimmed. Ease them out. As the sails begin to work better, the boat will accelerate.

Broad reaching is easy on the crew. With the wind at your back, the boat doesn't heel, no spray comes on board, and it feels warmer. This makes it a good point of sail to be on when you want to take a break, perhaps to open up a cold drink or have a sandwich.

TIP *On a broad reach or run, the normal signs of correct sail trim — that bubbling at the luff — are very subtle or nonexistent. This is because the sails are working more like those old square-rigger sails with the wind pushing them rather than flowing across their airfoil surface. For best power on these points of sail, ease the boom out until it's almost perpendicular to the wind direction (but don't let it rest on the shrouds). Because the jib has no boom that runs into the shrouds, it can be eased more than the mainsail so, as you ease, you might see that small luff starting at the leading edge.*

Sail trim on a broad reach is more difficult to call. When you ease the mainsheet well out, the sail begins to lie on the leeward shrouds.

WIND
DIRECTION

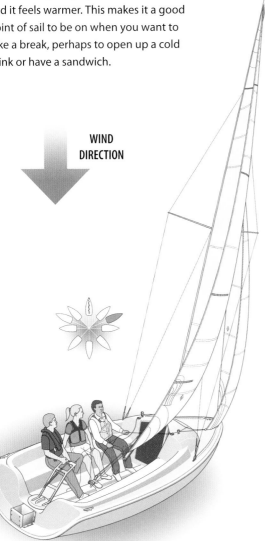

④ **CLOSE REACH**

⑤ **BROAD REACH**

IT'S ALL ABOUT THE WIND

A sailor's life revolves around the wind. Its direction and its strength govern where he can sail, with what degree of difficulty or comfort, and how quickly. Naturally, the language of sailing reflects how sailors orient themselves and everything around them with reference to the wind.

UPWIND AND DOWNWIND

The sailor's world is roughly divided into two hemispheres: upwind and downwind. Anywhere or anything in the direction from which the wind is blowing is upwind; anywhere or anything in the direction toward which it's blowing is downwind.

When sailing, you trim the sails according to the wind direction relative to the boat. You first encountered the all-important "points of sail" in Chapter 1. Now that you're out on the water, you'll be constantly aware of them as the wind changes and as your course changes too. You will continually fine-tune the trim of your sails to suit the degree to which you are sailing upwind or downwind.

By understanding the points of sail and their implications on crew comfort and sail trim, the helmsman and the crew will be able to work together to move the boat efficiently to any destination they choose.

SAILING CLOSE-HAULED

You sail close-hauled on the very edge of the no-sail-zone — making your best speed toward a destination to windward. This involves a balancing act between boat speed and your course, or angle to the wind. For most boats, that angle is about 45 degrees to the true-wind direction, but it varies with the design of the boat, the shape of the sails (both their geometry and physical condition!), and the strength of the wind.

If you attempt to sail a course *above* close-hauled, or closer to the wind, the sails will no longer deliver full power and the boat will slow down. Sailing a course

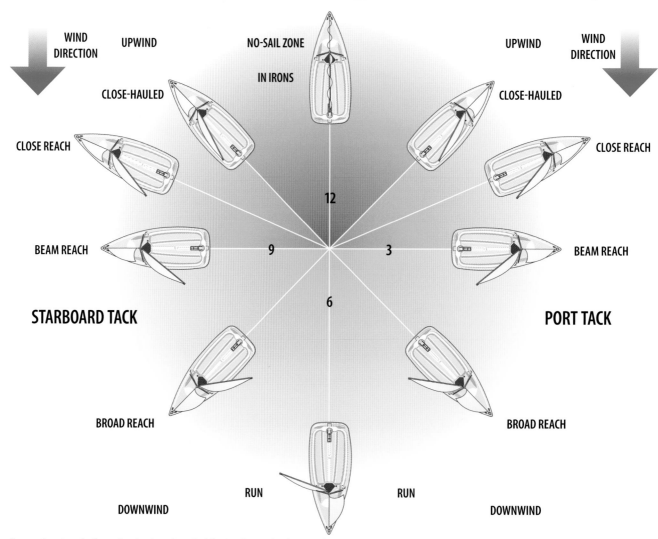

Because the points of sail are referred to throughout the following chapters, here's a reminder.

When sailing close-hauled, the goal is to achieve the best trim possible for the sails and then steer to the sails, keeping the boat in the groove. In all but the lightest winds, the boat will heel noticeably, adding to the sensation of speed.

TIP *Re-check halyard tension while sailing close-hauled.*

PROBLEM *Vertical wrinkles indicate too much halyard tension.*

SOLUTION *Carefully ease halyard tension one inch at a time until they disappear.*

PROBLEM *Scallops between hanks or loose horizontal wrinkles along the luff indicate too little luff tension.*

SOLUTION *Ease the jibsheet or head up a little until the sail luffs and add halyard tension one inch at a time.*

So now you're in the groove, but don't get too comfortable. You're trying to get to windward, and there's only one way to get there and that's by a series of changes in course.

below close-hauled (or *footing off*), would be faster but, if your destination is upwind, you would not be making as much progress toward it. Close-hauled is that happy confluence of speed and course that brings the boat upwind with maximum efficiency. Many sailors find close-hauled the most enjoyable point of sail. The wind (this is the apparent wind, remember) will feel the strongest in the crew's faces, while the boat bounces along merrily over the waves (maybe sending a bit of spray on deck) heeling more than on any other point of sail. All of this adds to the exhilaration and fun of sailing.

Start on a beam reach and head up about 45 degrees. Concurrently trim the jibsheet tightly (but not rock hard). Trim the mainsail to the point that its luff just stops bubbling. The boom will lie a little off centerline. Experiment with small changes to the trim of both sails — it's a fine art!

Steering is especially important when sailing close-hauled because with the sails pulled in tight there's no more to trim in. The driver must be constantly adjusting course to any shifts of wind.

Short dark yarns or nylon strips streaming on the jib a foot or two back from the luff — *telltales* — are an excellent close-hauled steering aid (see page 62).

TIP *Except in very light winds, when the boat is barely moving, the helmsman, whether using a tiller or a wheel, should always sit on the windward side for visibility and control.*

When you're steering just a little too close to the wind, or *pinching*, the warning signs are obvious: The jib begins to luff at its leading edge, signaling your entry into the no-sail zone. When you steer just slightly lower than your optimum close-hauled course, the sails will look full but you are no longer making your best speed to windward. Get in the groove! Concentrate on steering as close to the wind as possible without causing that small luff in the front of the jib with its associated loss of speed.

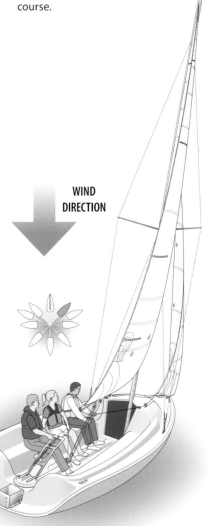

WIND DIRECTION

CLOSE-HAULED

TACKING — GETTING FROM ZIG TO ZAG AND BACK

A sailboat cannot make any forward progress directly into the wind. When you tried to sail too close to the wind, the sails simply flapped and you lost headway. You may even have put the boat in irons. To reach a destination directly upwind, you have to sail a zigzag course. Each leg of the zigzag will be approximately 45 degrees away from the direct line between your starting point and your destination. Think of climbing up a mountain on a trail with a series of switchbacks. This means at some point, you have to get from your zig course to your zag course, which is on the other side of the no-sail zone.

TACKING DEFINED

When you turn the boat so that its bow passes entirely through the wind — that is, through the no-sail zone — that's called *tacking*. The word tack gets a bit of a workout here, just as you will when you tack the boat.

When the boat is sailing with the wind blowing on the starboard side, it's on *starboard tack*, and when the wind is blowing on the port side, the moving sailboat is on *port tack*. To reach a destination directly toward the wind, you have to sail, using the steering skills you just learned, part of the way close-hauled on starboard tack and part of the way close-hauled on port tack. To bring the boat from close-hauled on starboard tack to close-hauled on port tack, you must pass through the no-sail zone — you have to tack.

TACK, TACKING, AND TACKS

If you take a breather here for a little mental exercise, you can see where the apparently multiple meanings of "tack" come from. An old-time square sail was supported along its top by a horizontal spar, or yard, and had control lines on the bottom two corners. When sailing close-hauled, one of those corners was hauled forward and down, and was therefore the tack of the sail, and the other was hauled aft. If the wind was on the starboard side, the starboard corner was the tack — starboard tack. To go from sailing with the wind on the ship's starboard side to sailing with it on the port side, the crew had to literally change tacks.

Now that we've cleared that up, we also use the term *coming about* to mean tacking.

TACKING A SAILBOAT

Tacking requires good teamwork from the entire crew. When you tack the boat, it must have enough momentum to carry it through the no-sail zone. So the boat doesn't slow down and get stuck in irons, you have to be at full speed going into the maneuver and turn steadily throughout the tack.

Make sure the boat is sailing on a close-hauled course and trim both sails so it's sailing efficiently — at full speed.

① Sitting on the windward side, the helmsman scans all around the boat, particularly ahead and abeam to windward, looking for obstructions or other boats in the way. When he is sure there is room for the maneuver, he alerts the crew by giving the command "Prepare to tack!" or the more traditional, "Ready about!"

TIP *During a tack, the mainsheet needs very little or even no adjustment if you want to keep things simple.*

② A crewmember takes up a position at each jibsheet and ensures that the tails of both sheets are clear and free to run.

TIP *On a smaller boat, one person can handle both jibsheets in a tack.*

③ The crew handling the working jibsheet prepares to release it. If it's on a winch, he can uncleat it, but must keep holding it tightly at the winch without easing it.

TIP *Never release the jibsheet while the sail is full and drawing — wait for the turn.*

④ The crew at the lazy sheet, which will become the working sheet on the new tack, pulls in any slack and puts one to three wraps around the winch depending on the wind speed and the size of the winch.

TIP *Remember too many wraps and you risk an override, too few and the sheet will pull out of your hands when the load increases.*

⑤ The helmsman waits for all crew to respond, "Ready!" then announces the beginning of the turn with a command like the classic, "Helm's a-lee," or, "Tacking," and pushes the tiller smoothly to leeward to initiate the turn.

TIP *The boom will always be pushed by the sail to the leeward side. To tack, (assuming you are sitting on the windward side of the cockpit) you push the tiller toward the boom. On a boat with a steering wheel, the helmsman initiates a tack by turning the top of the wheel toward the wind.*

⑥ Watch the jib. As the boat turns up into the no-sail zone it will luff more and more until it is completely flapping — before it fills with wind on the opposite side. When it just begins luffing, the load on the sheet will lessen. At that moment, release it quickly and completely. This jibsheet now becomes the lazy sheet.

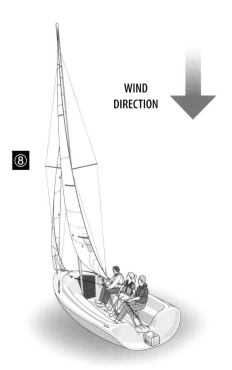

**WIND
DIRECTION**

⑧

⑦

America's Cup Class yachts strike a classic pose
crossing tacks as they race to windward.

⑥

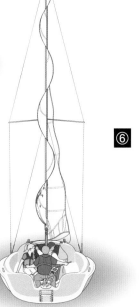

Simultaneously, the crew on the old lazy
sheet quickly takes up all the slack while
the sail is fully luffing as the boat's bow
passes through the *eye of the wind.*

TIP *Turn at a consistent rate — do not slow
down or stop the turn until you are nearly on
the new close-hauled course! If you turn too
slowly, the boat will lose momentum and
may not make it onto the new tack. Turn too
sharply and the crew might not have time to
perform their duties, or the boat might
overshoot the desired new heading.*

⑦ Having moved across the boat to the
"new" windward side during the turn, the
helmsman centers the tiller or wheel to
stop the turn with the boat close-hauled
on the new tack.

TIP *Before the tack it's helpful to pick a
landmark about 90 degrees to windward
and use it as a reference so you stop the turn
on the proper close-hauled course.*

⑧ Trim the new working jibsheet for the
new course — if it's windy, you may need
the winch handle. The mainsail, which
was trimmed for close-hauled on the
other tack, should need little if any trim
adjustment on the new tack.

⑨ The cockpit crew coil their sheets, the
winch handle is removed and stowed,

and the helmsman
concentrates on
rebuilding the speed
lost during the turn.

During a tack, everyone apart
from the two jibsheet crew moves
from the old windward side of the boat
to the new one. Exactly when they do so
depends on the layout of the cockpit, but
everyone should be in their new
positions by the time the boat has settled
on the new tack. The key is to coordinate
movements so as not to interfere with
the helmsman or trimmers and to stay
clear of the boom and mainsheet.

Tacking with both mainsail and jib
requires coordination and planning.
It can be noisy when the sails are
flapping, and the boat will start out
heeling one way and finish heeling
the other — it all may seem a bit
chaotic. With practice, though,
any crew can refine the timing
and trimming to the point that
it becomes automatic. Tacking
practice is a great way to build
a crew's teamwork.

While steering the boat through the
tack, the helmsman crosses from the
old windward side to the new one. The
crew follow once they have completed
their tasks.

①

JIBING — CHANGING TACKS THE OTHER WAY

So, we've made a few tacks and have gained considerable distance to windward. Now we have to get back to where we started from, and the most direct way is by running — which comes from running before the wind. The old square riggers were designed primarily for this point of sail, but it's a little trickier in a modern boat, as we'll see.

RUNNING

When you are sailing with the wind more or less directly behind the boat, at six o'clock on the points-of-sail diagram, you are running. There is no exact line of demarcation between broad reaching and running: It falls somewhere in the region where the jib collapses, blanketed by the mainsail.

When running, more than on any other point of sail, the helmsman has to be on his toes. A slight lapse of attention can result in an accidental *jibe*, which, if it's windy, could cause damage to the boat and injury to crew. For this reason, many sailors prefer to avoid sailing dead downwind and instead head up just 10 degrees or so to a broad reach where the risk of an accidental jibe is much diminished and the jib will fill. So, before we try sailing on a run, we'll stick to broad reaching.

We might not be able to sail to our destination on one broad reach, and at some point we'll have to jibe onto the other tack. But by jibing from broad reach to broad reach, we'll ensure our jibe is intentional and controlled — the way we would like every jibe to be.

JIBING DEFINED

Like a tack, a jibe is a maneuver in which the boat changes tacks (the side of the boat upon which the wind blows). In a jibe, the boat turns away from the wind — from 5 o'clock to 7 o'clock (or vice versa) at the downwind side of the points-of-sail diagram. Unconstrained by the no-sail zone, the boat can be turned through a smaller arc and is powered forward by the wind throughout the maneuver, except in the moment when the wind gets behind the mainsail and blows it, often suddenly and with great force, from one side of the boat to the other. To ensure smooth execution of a jibe, the helmsman and crew have to coordinate their actions closely.

JIBING WITH MAINSAIL AND JIB

When you tacked, the mainsail was trimmed in tight. You could almost ignore it while giving your attention to tacking the jib. When jibing, your focus is on the mainsail and controlling its movement across the boat. The jib, partially blanketed by the mainsail through most of the maneuver, is much easier to handle in a jibe. Here are the steps to a jibe, from broad reach to broad reach, in our small keelboat in light to moderate winds.

① Start on a broad reach with both sails trimmed correctly. Station a crew at each jibsheet and at the mainsheet.

② After checking that the water ahead is clear, the helmsman gives the command "Prepare to jibe!" or words to that effect.

③ The crew on the working jibsheet prepares to release the sheet, just as when tacking, except there will be very little load on the sheet. The crew on the lazy sheet, on our small keelboat likely the same person, hauls in all the slack and takes a couple of wraps on the winch. When ready, they and the mainsheet trimmer respond by saying clearly, "Ready."

④ Everyone on board should take positions out of the way of the mainsheet and below the path the boom will take during the jibe.

⑤ The helmsman, sitting to windward still, then calls out, "Jibe-ho," or, "Jibing," and begins to turn the boat slowly away from the wind by pulling the tiller toward him or turning the wheel in the direction the boat is to turn.

⑥ The mainsheet trimmer hauls in fast on the sheet while keeping the tail clear and ready to be eased back out after the jibe. As soon as the jib collapses, the crew on the new working jibsheet takes in slack and the old jibsheet is cast off.

Running in a strong breeze is exhilarating and fast, but the helmsman must give the steering his full attention.

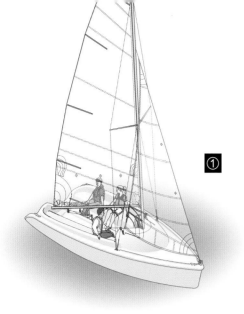

①

WIND DIRECTION

⑥

⑦ As the boat turns past dead-downwind, the wind will catch the back side of the mainsail and push it across to the other side with tremendous force. The mainsheet crew must quickly but carefully allow the mainsheet to run out until the mainsail is set correctly for a broad reach on the new tack.

TIP *In stronger winds, if the sail is not let out quickly as soon as the main and boom "flop" over, the newly filled mainsail will cause the boat to heel and* round up *toward the wind. When helmsman and mainsheet trimmer work closely together, a jibe can be an elegant maneuver. When they don't, the mainsail can become unruly.*

⑧ Once on a broad reach on the new tack, the helmsman changes to the new windward side and centers the helm. The crew trim the sails for the new heading.

TIP *The helmsman's role is crucial in the jibe, preparing the crew with commands and turning the boat slowly — more slowly than in a tack — yet steadily all the way through the jibe.*

TIP *On a boat with wheel steering, standing or sitting behind the wheel is fine on downwind courses and often gives the helmsman better control.*

The optimal speed at which to turn and the timing of when you shift the sails will vary from boat to boat and depends on the conditions. In our example, we went from broad reach to broad reach — about a 30-degree turn. Although technically you could jibe from beam reach to beam reach, a 180-degree turn, it's far easier on the crew and boat to limit the amount of the turn in the jibe. You can always turn up to a tighter reach after the jibe is complete as an additional step.

In stronger winds, it might be prudent to forgo the stress and danger of a jibe and change tacks the "easier" way — by tacking.

⑦

⑧

When jibing, the helmsman and mainsheet trimmer must coordinate their actions closely. The jib trimmer has an easier job than in a tack, but must watch for the boom as it crosses the cockpit.

When the wind is blowing from directly astern, it's possible to sail wing-on-wing. When doing so, the helmsman must pay close attention to the wind direction.

SAILING WING-ON-WING

Now that we've been through a jibe or two, you know why you don't want one to sneak up on you while you're sailing on a *dead run*, with the wind dead astern.

When running, your goal is to sail with the wind blowing directly over the stern, to hold the wind there, and to not turn any farther downwind and risk a jibe. Before you turn the boat on to a run, make sure you have a good feel for the wind direction and that the entire crew is below the plane of the boom and out of the way of the path of the mainsheet and vang should you jibe.

① Start from a broad reach with the boom vang snug and cleated and turn

**WIND
DIRECTION**

When sailing wing-on-wing, the jib and mainsail are set on opposite sides of the boat.

gradually downwind until the jib collapses because it has become blanketed from the wind by the mainsail.

② Ease the mainsheet all the way until the boom almost hits the shrouds.

....

TIP *On a run, the sail will not luff, because the wind is pushing straight on it and not flowing across it. Your best indicator of sail trim is to set the boom perpendicular to the wind direction.*

....

③ Release the old leeward, working jibsheet and pull the windward jibsheet until the clew comes across and the sail fills with wind on the opposite side —to windward.

④ When sailing dead downwind like this, the helmsman needs to steer very carefully and very straight to avoid an accidental jibe and to keep the wind filling the jib. Concentrate! Use a far-off landmark as a reference to steer straight and be attuned to the feel of the wind direction on your skin.

....

TIP *A wind vane at the top of the mast or yarn telltales flying from the shrouds or the backstay can be really helpful references when running.*

....

You are now *winging the jib*, or sailing *wing-on-wing*, and this is the only point of sail where the main and jib will set on opposite sides. You may need to hold the jibsheet out to help keep the jib flying. Bigger boats sometimes employ a strut or pole to hold the clew in place.

SAILING BY THE LEE

When running dead downwind, you must be careful that the wind does not shift, or that you do not lose your concentration and allow the boat to turn slightly so that the wind is coming across the "wrong" side of the boat — from the same side as the mainsail. This is called *sailing by the lee*, and it can be very dangerous, especially in stronger winds, because you

are right on the edge of an accidental jibe. It should be avoided because of the potential for damage and injury. If the mainsail leech begins to curl to windward, that's your warning sign that you are sailing by the lee and an accidental jibe is imminent. Turn the boat immediately back toward your original broad reaching course—tiller toward the boom; top of the wheel away from the boom.

....

TIP *If you do notice an accidental jibe occurring, yell "duck" loudly to warn the crew that the boom and its associated rigging is going to be coming across the cockpit with a vengeance.*

....

**WIND
DIRECTION**

When sailing by the lee, the wind is on the same side of the boat as the mainsail.

REVIEW QUESTIONS (see page 126 for answers)

FILL IN THE BLANK OR MATCH THE LETTER WITH THE WORD

1 The mainsail should be raised when the sailboat is oriented _____ to _____.

2 When turning the boat toward the wind, the sails should be _____ in.

3 When turning the boat away from the wind, the sails should be _____ out.

4 "Fluttering" sails are said to be _____.

5 The best way to steer the boat on a straight course is to look toward the _____ and pick a _____ to steer toward.

6 When you turn the bow of the boat toward the wind you are _____ _____.

7 When you turn the bow of the boat away from the wind you are _____ _____.

8 The "golden rule" of sail trim is: "when in _____, let it _____."

9 When the boat is stopped, pointed toward the wind with the sails luffing, it is said to be _____ _____.

10 Match the points of sail with the letters in the illustration:
- ☐ In irons/no-sail zone
- ☐ Close-hauled
- ☐ Close reach
- ☐ Beam reach
- ☐ Broad reach
- ☐ Run

11 When the wind is blowing on the port side, the boat is said to be sailing on a _____ _____.

12 When the wind is blowing on the starboard side, the boat is said to be sailing on a _____ _____.

13 Turning the boat so the bow passes through the wind, bringing the wind to blow onto the opposite side of the boat, is called _____.

14 Changing tacks by turning the boat so its stern passes through the wind is called _____.

15 The helmsman's commands for tacking the boat (also called "coming about") are "_____ _____" and "_____ _____."

16 The helmsman's commands for jibing the boat are "_____ to _____" and "_____-_____."

17 To jibe safely, it's very important to _____ the _____ in toward the centerline as the boat bears away onto a run.

18 Sailing on a run with the mainsail and jib on opposite sides of the boat is called sailing _____ -on-_____.

19 If the wind is on the same side of the boat as the mainsail while sailing downwind, the boat is said to be _____ by the _____.

20 The danger of sailing by the lee is the increased risk of an _____ _____.

10 Points of Sail

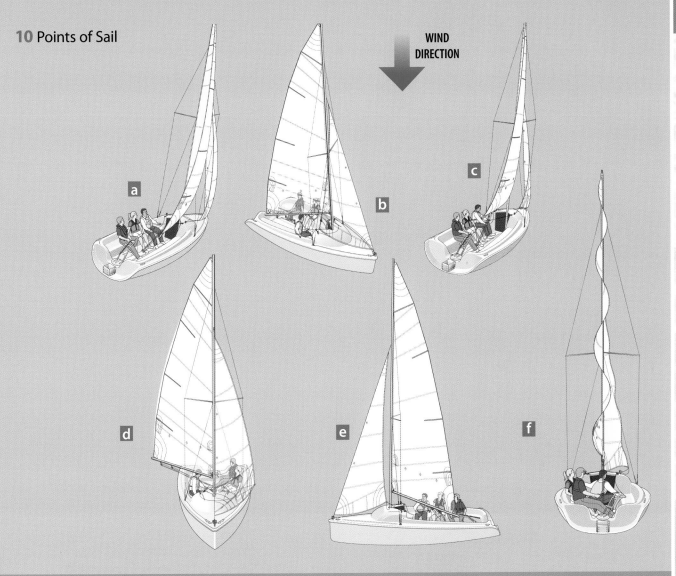

WIND
DIRECTION

NOTES

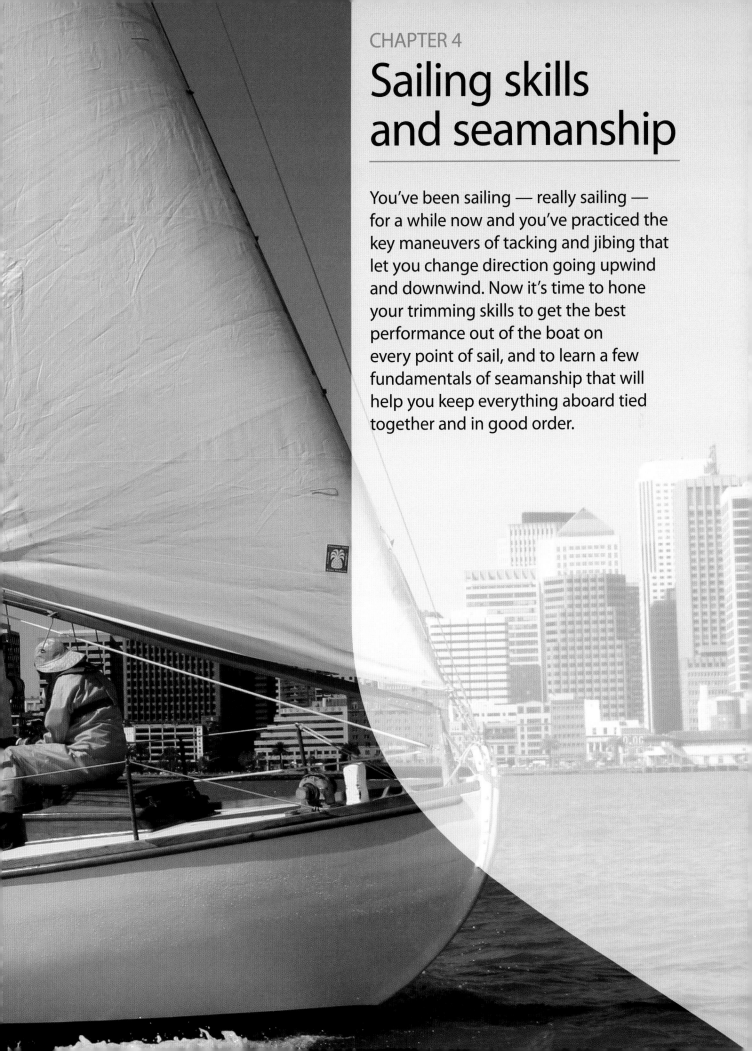

CHAPTER 4

Sailing skills and seamanship

You've been sailing — really sailing — for a while now and you've practiced the key maneuvers of tacking and jibing that let you change direction going upwind and downwind. Now it's time to hone your trimming skills to get the best performance out of the boat on every point of sail, and to learn a few fundamentals of seamanship that will help you keep everything aboard tied together and in good order.

BETTER SAILING

In Chapter 1, you learned some sailing theory and had your first lesson in the language of boats. In Chapter 2, you set the sails, and in Chapter 3, you put some of that theory to practice and used the language to communicate with your fellow crewmembers. You have a feel for the wind and for the boat, and how you can capture the energy of one and use it to drive the other. Now is a good time to broaden your understanding of some of the basic concepts, such as sail trim, and to learn a few sailors' techniques for securing all those lines we have on board.

BETTER SAIL TRIM

Sails transfer energy from the wind to the boat. How efficiently they convert the wind's force into forward motion depends on how they are trimmed. A sail's trim is a combination of the angle at which it is set to the wind, over which we have a lot of control, and its aerodynamic shape, over which we have a limited amount of control.

In general, in light winds (under 5 knots), you want your sails to obtain the maximum power out of what little wind there is. As the breeze increases, it will reach a point where more energy is available than the boat can utilize for forward motion. When this happens, the boat will heel too much and you'll want to begin "de-powering" the sails to achieve the best speed. Once the wind is up in the moderate range (6 to 12 knots) you generally want more "powerful" sails when sailing on a reach or run and less powerful sails when sailing upwind. At certain times,

such as when approaching a dock under sail, you will want to intentionally slow down and control your speed.

The simplest and fastest way to adjust a sail's power is to change its angle to the wind by adjusting the sheet, which is why you can think of the sheet of a sail as its gas pedal. You can also turn the boat, but that means you might not be heading in the direction you want to go.

The aerodynamic shape of the sail has a lesser but still important effect on the sail's power. Much of that shape was built in by the sailmaker, but you can tweak it by adjusting the secondary sail controls: the outhaul, the Cunningham/downhaul, the halyard, and the boom vang.

THE UNDER-TRIMMED SAIL

When a sail is under-trimmed, it will generate less than optimum power. This will be the case if its sheet has been eased too far for the present wind angle. The obvious indicator of an under-

trimmed sail is luffing, which will appear first as a "bubble" along the leading edge of the sail. When it luffs, the sail loses power and the boat will slow down and tend to heel less. Easing the sheet more will cause the luffing area to spread over more of the sail.

When a sail is under-trimmed, you can power it up by either sheeting in or by turning the boat away from the wind until the sail just stops luffing.

....

TIP *These rules apply in most conditions, but remember, a mainsail cannot luff when sailing on a run. In really strong winds, letting your sails luff just a little when they would otherwise be overpowered will let you sail faster because too much heel slows the boat.*

....

Releasing the sails' sheets while steering straight is a great way to intentionally slow the boat down.

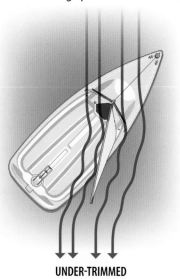

UNDER-TRIMMED

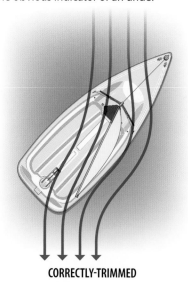

CORRECTLY-TRIMMED

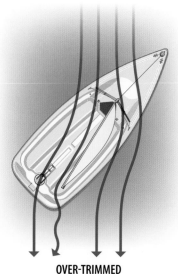

OVER-TRIMMED

When a sail is trimmed correctly, so that its airfoil shape is working at its highest efficiency, the wind flows smoothly around it creating maximum driving force and minimum drag.

THE OVER-TRIMMED SAIL

When a sail is over-trimmed, it generates less power even while it looks full. The wind hits the sail at too wide an angle, disrupting the wind flow and, like a stalled airplane wing, the sail generates less lift and more drag.

The signs of over-trim are less obvious than the signs of under-trim. If you think a sail might be over-trimmed, apply the golden rule of sail trim: "When in doubt, ease it out." If the sail starts to luff as soon as you ease it, the trim was already correct. If it takes a lot of easing before it begins to luff, it was over-trimmed. To get full power, trim the sail just enough to stop it from luffing. Of course, another way to bring the sail to the correct angle to the wind would be to change the angle of the boat by heading up toward the wind.

....

TIP *Whenever you have any doubt about a sail's trim, ease the sail and see what happens.*

....

SHAPING THE MAINSAIL

A sailmaker can build "shape" into an apparently flat sail by varying the widths of the fabric panels and with other techniques. Once the sail is hoisted, the crew can further tweak the sail's shape.

An important feature of a sail is its *draft*, the depth and shape of the curve that makes it look like an airfoil. Simply put, more draft means more power. In strong winds, much of that power will be trying to push the boat sideways rather than forward. To reduce power, you reduce the draft to make the sail flatter.

Adding tension to the outhaul flattens the sail. Adding tension to the halyard flattens the sail and also moves the draft forward, and with it the effective center of the sail's driving force. A Cunningham lets you tension the luff of the sail without using the halyard. On some boats, the backstay is adjustable. This lets you alter the shape of the sail by bending the mast.

The boom vang restrains the boom from rising up and thereby controls the tension in the leech of the mainsail and the degree to which the upper part of the leech twists off. The boom vang is especially useful off the wind. On a boat that doesn't have a mainsheet traveler, it also helps control the leech when sailing on the wind.

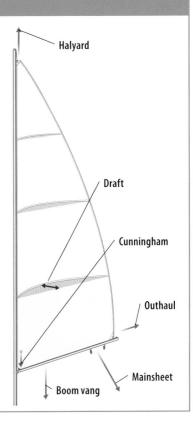

Halyard

Draft

Cunningham

Outhaul

Mainsheet

Boom vang

When sailing close-hauled, once the sails have been trimmed to get the best performance in the conditions, it's up to the helmsman to steer to the sails while the crew acts as ballast.

SAILING "IN THE GROOVE"

You trim and ease a sail to get the wind to flow across it smoothly. That would be a lot easier to do if you could see the wind. The next best thing is to attach something to the sail that will show you what's happening to the air flow across it. That something is a *telltale*.

SAILING TO TELLTALES

Telltales, usually made of short lengths of colored yarn or ribbon, provide the sail trimmers and helmsman with invaluable visual input on the state of a sail's trim. On jibs, they work so well that they are arguably essential equipment. They are attached near the luff on either side of the jib about a foot back from the forestay, starting at about 4 feet up from the tack and often at several higher levels. The sail cloth is usually translucent enough that you can see both the windward and leeward telltales.

When these luff telltales on both sides of the jib flow back horizontally, the air is flowing smoothly and the sail is performing efficiently. A telltale fluttering on one side of the sail shows that the air is being disrupted by over-trim or under-trim.

Telltales are especially useful for the helmsman when sailing upwind, and are a great reference

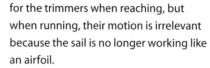

for the trimmers when reaching, but when running, their motion is irrelevant because the sail is no longer working like an airfoil.

When sailing upwind, the helmsman should glance at the jib telltales (the lower ones are the best for a steering reference) every 10 seconds or so to ensure the boat is sailing in the close-hauled "groove" with the jib working efficiently.

READING THE TELLTALES

Let's assume the boat is sailing upwind in a steady light-to-medium wind. It's not overpowered and heeling too much and the jibsheet is properly trimmed and cleated for sailing close-hauled. Here's how the telltales give their feedback.
① If the boat is sailing the optimum close-hauled course, the telltales will be streaming back along the surface of the sail — you're "in the groove!"
② Very slowly, head up, turning the boat toward the wind about 5 degrees. The windward telltale (on the "inside" of the sail) will begin to "dance," rising up. The leeward telltale will keep streaming. If you keep heading up, the luff of the jib will begin to bubble too, but the telltale reacts to under-trim sooner — it's your early-warning indicator.
③ Gradually turn the boat away from the

wind until you're back in the groove with both telltales streaming evenly.
④ Now very slowly bear away. Soon the leeward (outside) telltale will begin to dance up and down while the windward one continues to flow straight. The sail still "looks" full, but that leeward telltale is warning us that the sail is over-trimmed. If we bear away 10 degrees or more below that optimum close-hauled course — the "groove" — both telltales will hang limply, indicating the sail is massively over-trimmed: We are steering way too low for the trim.
⑤ Slowly head back up until the telltales signal that you are back "in the groove."

On a reach, the helmsman may decide to steer a straight course, in which case the jib-luff telltales will provide the same accurate, "early warning" feedback of improper trim to the sail trimmers. If the windward telltale dances, trim the jibsheet slightly until both are streaming back. If the leeward telltale begins to jump around, ease the sheet a bit.

On a mainsail, telltales are nowhere near as valuable as they are on the jib, because they don't work well near the luff where the mast causes turbulence in the airflow. When they are used, they are attached to the leech, where they provide valuable information about the airflow coming off the sail.

Some racing sails have a window in the luff to give the helmsman a clearer view of the leeward telltale.

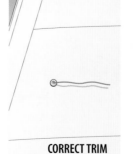

CORRECT TRIM

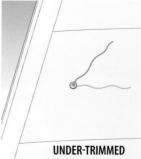

UNDER-TRIMMED

OVER-TRIMMED

Telltales near the luff of the jib provide the best guide to sail trim and, when close-hauled, help the helmsman keep the boat sailing "in the groove." The sailcloth is usually translucent enough for the helmsman to see the leeward telltale.

STEERING AND TRIM IN STRONGER WINDS

Although the focus of this book and the ASA101 Basic Keelboat Sailing Standard is on learning to sail in light to moderate winds, you may run into breezy conditions early in your sailing career. Sailing in stronger breezes is fun, if the boat and crew are prepared for the extra horsepower. (The power of the wind goes up by the square of its velocity, so 20 knots of breeze packs four times the punch of 10 knots). As you progress through the ASA system of certification, you will learn how to prepare a boat and safely sail it in rough conditions. For now, here's a taste of how an increase in wind will affect your steering and your sail trimming.

Whitecaps on the water are a sign of a fresh breeze. To handle it, this boat is carrying a reef in the mainsail to reduce sail area.

CONTROLLING HEEL

When sailing in stronger winds, the boat will heel more, especially when close-hauled — the "tippiest" point of sail — and also when on a close or a beam reach. How much heel is right? On a dinghy, the optimum heel is less than 10 degrees (and the crew hang out over the windward side to restrict the heeling). On a keelboat, it depends on your boat, but in general, if the boat heels more than 15 to 20 degrees it will be difficult to steer straight because the combination of wind and heel create significant turning forces which usually try to make the boat head up into the wind. You feel them as *weather helm* when the tiller (or wheel) resists your efforts to steer away from the wind.

TIP *When a boat carries a little weather helm, it's considered a good quality. It gives the helmsman a positive feel and ensures that if he has to leave the helm to tend to something else, the boat will head up and slow down. A boat with lee helm will tend to turn downwind and perhaps even jibe, which is not at all desirable.*

Here are a few ways you can keep the heeling under control when the wind comes up, in the general order of how you would apply them:

■ Move all the crew to the windward side of the boat.
■ Tighten the mainsail outhaul and increase luff tension on mainsail and jib.
■ When sailing close-hauled, steer the

boat slightly closer to the wind so the sails are slightly under-trimmed. (Let the windward telltale dance.)
■ Depower the mainsail. The general rule is to depower your sail plan from back to front, so start by easing the mainsheet or traveler.

TIP *There's a difference between sailing in consistent strong winds and just experiencing the occasional gust on an otherwise moderate day. The steps above will help you react to these short gusts. It can really help to have a dedicated person on the mainsheet or traveler ready to ease quickly in the puff, and then bring it back in quickly when the puff goes away.*

■ If after taking all these steps the boat is still overpowered and heeling too much, it's probably time to take the more drastic step of reducing sail area. The easiest way to do this is by dropping the jib (or rolling it up if it's on a furler),

WATCH FOR SIGNS OF WIND

One of the best ways to estimate wind strength is to look at the surface of the water. The more wind, the more agitated it gets and the degrees by which it does so are so predictable that they are tabulated in the Beaufort Wind Scale, which is discussed in *Coastal Cruising Made Easy*. The more time you spend sailing, the more you will begin to recognize the signs of too little, just enough, and too much wind.

because keelboats usually sail better under mainsail alone than under jib alone.
■ Change to a smaller jib if your boat has one. Some boats have several jibs of different sizes to suit various wind conditions.
■ Reduce mainsail area by *reefing*.

WHAT IS REEFING?

When you *reef* a sail, you make it smaller so that less area is exposed to the wind, thus reducing the force acting on the sail.

To reef the mainsail, you lower it part way and attach it by a "new" tack and clew a little way above the normal tack and clew. Several different methods are used for reefing mainsails and they require practice to perform smoothly in strong winds.

Some jibs that are on roller furlers can be reefed by rolling them up a little. Otherwise, jibs are not customarily reefed — when the wind gets too strong, you drop the jib and hoist a smaller one.

Reefing and other techniques for sailing in heavy weather are covered in *Coastal Cruising Made Easy*.

TIP *Avoid sailing on a run in strong winds — steering becomes difficult and you are just too close to an accidental jibe. Head up to a broad reach so you have better steering control.*

TYING IT ALL TOGETHER

Through most of the age of sail, ships and their spars were made of wood and all rigging, running and standing alike, was made of rope. To connect it all together, riggers and seamen devised hundreds of knots, bends, hitches, and splices. Most standing rigging on modern sailboats is made of wire, and attached to hull, deck, and spars with mechanical connections. But because the dock lines and most of the sail controls, like the mainsheet, are made of rope, you still need to know a few basic but versatile knots. A common characteristic of the knots you will learn here is that they are easy to tie and relatively easy to untie (some more so than others) even after they have been under load. Knowing these knots will make life afloat easier and safer, and you might also find them valuable at times even when you are not sailing.

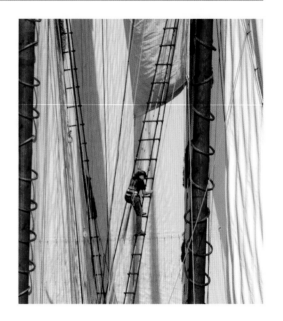

A FEW SIMPLE SAILOR'S KNOTS

A whole subset of language has developed around rope and the countless ways in which it can be tied. Knots, bends, and hitches are used to tie rope to itself, to other ropes, and to solid objects; splices involve using the component parts of the rope itself to similar ends. Any serious sailor should have a book of knots in his library, but here we'll stick with a few common terms that aid in describing how to make the basic sailor's knots.

When you're making a knot, the length of rope you hold in your hand is called the *working part*. The end of the rope you are working with is called the *bitter end*. The rest of the rope, between the working part and its other end, whether it's faked at your feet or tied to something on the boat, is called the *standing part*.

BOWLINE

One of the most beautiful and useful sailing knots is the *bowline*, (pronounced "BO'lin"). The bowline forms a temporary eye, or loop, in the end of a line and is commonly used to attach a jibsheet to the clew of the jib.

① Make a small hole with a twist of the line so that the working part lies on top of the standing part. (In a popular method of teaching a bowline, this is the "rabbit hole.") How far from the bitter end you make this hole dictates how big the finished knot's loop will be.
② Pass the end up through the loop, under and around the standing part and back down through the loop. (The rabbit comes up the hole, around the tree and back down the hole again.)
③ Firm up the knot by pulling at the same time on the eye you made and on the standing part.

When attaching a jibsheet to the clew of a jib, between stage 1 and stage 2, pass the bitter end through the clew ring.

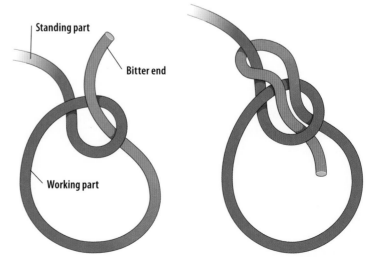

Standing part

Bitter end

Working part

FIGURE-EIGHT KNOT

This knot is fun to tie and can save you a lot of hassle. It's commonly tied at the bitter end of halyards and sheets to prevent them from getting inadvertently pulled out of the blocks, fairleads, and jammers they've been led through. Like its cousin the common overhand knot, the figure eight is bulky, and serves well as a stopper knot. Unlike its cousin, it is easily untied.

① Make a small loop near the end of the line. (Once the knot's complete, it's nice to have about 6 inches between it and the bitter end. This extra line gives you something to grab onto and ensures the knot won't come undone accidentally.)

② Pass the end of the line around the standing part and then back up and through the loop.

③ Pull both ends tight to firm up the knot.

This is a very easy knot to tie and once you've done it a few times you'll figure out your own way of doing it.

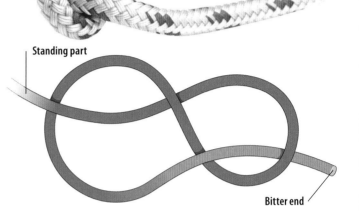

Standing part

Bitter end

CLEAT HITCH

Many working lines on a sailboat are secured on a horn or T cleat with this hitch. You will also use it to tie mooring lines to dock cleats.

Sometimes when tying a cleat hitch, there will already be load on the standing part of the line. The job of the hitch is to transfer that load from your hand to the cleat.

① Take a full turn around the base of the cleat so that the working part (in your hand) has passed under both horns. (If you expect a lot of load on the line and the cleat is big enough, add another half turn on the base for good measure).

② Wrap the working end up and diagonally across the top of the cleat and under the opposite horn.

③ Bring the end back diagonally across the first wrap (making an "X" over the center of the cleat).

You can visualize steps 2 and 3 as making a figure eight around the cleat.

④ Repeat 2, but this time tuck the working part under itself to make the hitch.

When you become adept, you'll flick the "locking tuck" in with a quick twist. If the line in question is one that will be watched and adjusted frequently (like a jibsheet), you could forgo that final locking tuck and instead simply add another full wrap or two around the base of the cleat.

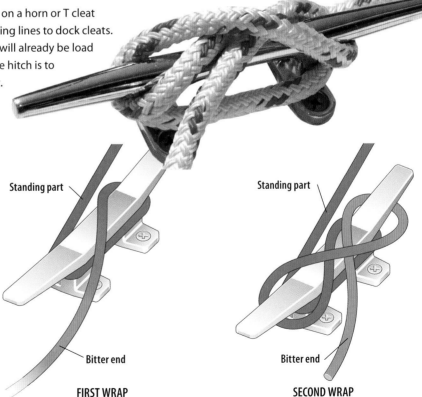

Standing part

Bitter end

FIRST WRAP

Standing part

Bitter end

SECOND WRAP

TIP *When the rope is made with some materials like natural-fibers, a highly loaded cleat hitch could bind so hard the only way to undo it is with a knife. Conversely, some modern synthetic ropes are so slippery that a simple cleat hitch won't hold. The solution to both problems is the same: Take another turn or two before making the locking turn.*

CLOVE HITCH

The clove hitch is usually employed for temporary needs. Using the clove hitch, you can quickly tie a line to a pole (such as a piling on a dock), a ring, or the standing part of another line. It's secure as long as it's under a constant load, but will work loose if subjected to on-and-off loads and can be difficult to untie under pressure, so it's rarely a preferred knot.

① Wrap the working end completely around the object you're tying to and cross it over the standing part.
② Wrap it around the object again, but this time on the opposite side of the standing part and tuck the tail through this turn.
③ Consolidate by tugging the tail tight so the two wraps are snug and together.

Bitter end

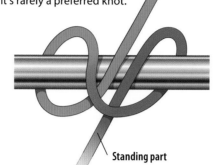

Standing part

ROUND TURN AND TWO HALF HITCHES

This may be the most underrated knot. It's fast to tie under load and applicable all around the boat. It's much more reliable and certainly easier to untie than its cousin the clove hitch. It can be tied into a ring or around a pole and it resists being shaken undone.

① With the working end, take a complete wrap around your object (if the line is under a lot of load, take two wraps to make tying it easier).
② Tie a *half hitch* (a simple overhand knot) around the standing part.
③ Tie a second half hitch around the standing part.
④ Consolidate by tugging on the bitter end.
If you look closely at your two half hitches, you'll see that they form a clove hitch around the standing part.

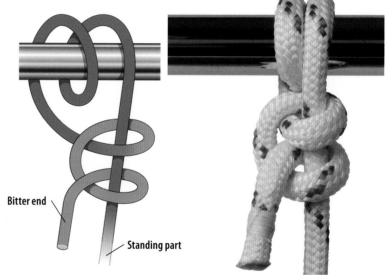

Bitter end

Standing part

SQUARE KNOT

Also called the reef knot, the square knot is well known to schoolchildren who have given up on trying to tie a bow in their shoelaces. On a boat it is used primarily for tying a rope to itself (such as when you are securing an item to the boat or to a spar).

① Take one end in each hand and pass one over and around the other to make a simple overhand knot.
② Cross the ends the opposite way to the first to make another overhand knot. If you put the left end over the right the first time, put the right end over the left to start the second overhand knot.
   A correct square knot is symmetrical, with each end lying next to, and on the same side of, its own standing part.

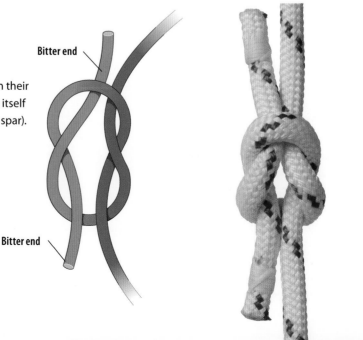

Bitter end

Bitter end

ROLLING HITCH

This valuable hitch can be used to tie a line to the standing part of another line or to a spar. It's especially useful when you need to transfer the load from one line to another — remember that winch override? It's similar to the clove hitch but with an extra turn on the side that's in the direction the load will be applied.

① Wrap the working end around the object you're tying to on the side toward the load.
② Make a second complete turn on the same side. When tying to a line, cross this second turn over the first. (When tying to a spar, don't cross these turns.)
③ Make a third turn, this time crossing over the standing part and finish the same way as for the clove hitch.

Bitter end

Standing part

VARIATIONS ON A THEME

Cleats are fittings that hold lines in place. They come in a variety of sizes and shapes but are usually of one of three basic types.

■ The horn cleat comes in many shapes and sizes. It holds a line very effectively, but making and releasing the needed cleat hitch takes a little time.

■ The cam cleat, which holds the line between spring-loaded jaws, is much faster to use. It's commonly found on dinghies and small keelboats, sometimes integrated with a block and tackle to allow quick adjustment to a mainsheet or a boom vang.

■ The jammer is like a super cam cleat with several moving parts including a lever that operates the internal mechanism that grips the line. Jammers can secure lines under very high load and are often used for securing halyards on bigger keelboats. Most jammers cannot be released when under load. The line must be tensioned on a winch and held there while the release lever is operated.

HORN CLEAT AS A MOORING CLEAT ON A YACHT

HORN CLEAT AS A MOORING CLEAT ON A DOCK

CAM CLEAT

CAM CLEAT USED WITH A MAINSHEET

JAMMER/ROPE CLUTCH

KEEPING THE BOAT SHIPSHAPE

As you have been finding out, sailboats are controlled by lines — lots of them and with many different functions. If not properly organized, these lines get tangled and mixed up, which can lead to confusion and create a hazard. Every line on a boat must therefore be kept tidy and in a designated place so that anyone can find it and work with it. Most lines that are not in active use are stowed in a neat coil. Active lines which have been cleated off (such as a halyard or a sheet) must also be made tidy by one of two methods: faking or coiling.

FAKING AND COILING

Faking is easy, and will quickly become an automatic response. As soon as you finish grinding in the jibsheet after a tack and you've stowed the winch handle, you fake out the tail of the sheet, back and forth, so it's ready to run free on the next tack.

Very often, the boat will have *tail bags* in the cockpit for active lines such as sheets and halyards. Start by simply putting the bitter end into the bottom of the bag, then slowly work the rest of the tail on top of it so that it comes out, you hope, as it went in — with no tangles.

When there is no tail bag, or you really want things tidy, you employ the coil. For example, once a sail has been hoisted, the tail of its halyard can be coiled and the coil hung nearby, on a cleat or on the winch, where it will be ready for action when the sail is dropped.

When a line will be infrequently needed, such as the halyard of a jib hoisted on a roller furler or a dock line being stowed away, then its coil should be secured by some finishing wraps as described below.

COILING A LINE

① Start at the working end, near the cleat, and take the line in one hand. You start at this end so any kinks will shake themselves out as you coil toward the bitter end. Move your other hand along the line until your hands are some intended distance apart — the longer and thicker the line, the greater the distance — and grasp the line at that point.
② Bring your hands together and transfer the point of the line held in your second hand to your first hand. You will now have a loop of the intended size of the coil.
③ Repeat the process until you have coiled the whole line into loops of equal length and are holding them in your first hand. If this is the jibsheet or mainsheet which is in use, you may simply lay the unfinished coil on deck at this point — making sure the bitter end doesn't go through the center of the coil and turn it all into a big knot!
④ You can tie the coil in a number of ways (and some skippers are particular about this), all of which require you to circle it. An easy way is to take the standing part, between the first loop of the coil and the cleat, and wrap it tightly around the coil, from the bottom toward the top. Three or four wraps should suffice, with the finishing wrap about a quarter of the way down from the top of the coil.
⑤ After the last wrap, grab the standing part just below the cleat and pull it through the coil. You now have a coiled line with its own hanger.

To finish a coil, wrap the standing part around the coil.

Push a bight of the standing part through the coil.

Pull the bight through the coil and use it as a hanger.

A FEW LINES ABOUT ROPE

Remember, rope is the raw material a sailor uses to make lines.

Most of the rope found on a modern sailboat is of braided construction. If you coil a braided-rope line consistently in one direction, you will introduce a twist in it which will cause it to kink when you want the line to run free. To avoid this, make the coils as figure eights. One way to do this is to hold the line in one hand and, with the other, pass the loops around a winch (which also helps you make all the loops the same size).

Modern synthetic materials allow rope manufacturers to impart characteristics almost at will, varying stretch, strength, diameter, color, and *hand* (how the rope feels) to suit any application. Our keelboat's halyards and sheets will probably be made of polyester (Dacron) fibers, but on bigger boats and racing boats where loads are higher you will hear names like Spectra, Kevlar, and Vectran.

Traditional rope is *laid up* of three or more strands twisted together in one direction. To prevent snarls, such rope should be coiled "with the *lay*," which is usually right handed. If you ever sail on a "tall ship," the mate will make sure that you do so.

Figure-eight coils don't always look perfectly neat, but they help prevent the line from becoming snarled as it runs out.

Three-strand rope is still widely used for dock and anchor lines as well as in running rigging on traditional craft.

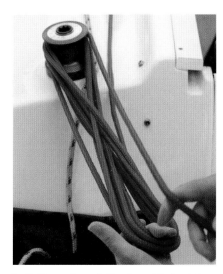

Braided lines are best coiled in a figure eight, for which an idle winch makes a handy helpmate.

FAKING FOR A DROP

A line that has been coiled, no matter how carefully, will always find a way to form a tangle when you want it to run free — Murphy lives for sailboats! To avoid this, for example when getting ready to drop a sail, fake (some say, flake) the halyard tail on the deck. Untie the "coiled halyard" and lay out the line on a flat surface in a tight zigzag. Start at the cleated end so any twists run out at the free end. The line will now run free without tangling — just don't stand on it!

When a lot of lines end up in one place, only tidy coils prevent an almighty tangle.

TAKING RESPONSIBILITY AFLOAT

In literature and in the movies, sailors are often depicted as being carefree and undisciplined. In real life, though, they do have responsibilites to each other, to their ship, and to other vessels. They are also subject to a degree of regulation, particularly when it comes to operating a boat when in the vicinity of other craft. Later on, in Chapter 6, we'll cover these regulations as they apply to our small keelboat. For now, it's enough to introduce some of the traditions of seafaring that will make you a better shipmate in any role you take aboard a sailboat.

ROLES OF SKIPPER AND CREW

All boats, however big or small, should operate under a very clear organizational structure with one leader. This individual, whether a professional captain in charge of a commercial vessel or the skipper of a recreational sailboat, bears the ultimate responsibility for the boat, its crew, and its actions on the water. Whoever assumes the role of skipper of a sailboat takes on the duty to know and obey any rules or laws that govern the boat and the body of water upon which it sails. In a sailing class, your instructor will probably take on this responsibility, which will still

be his even while, for teaching purposes, he lets you "act" as skipper. When you take a boat out without someone already designated as skipper, you assume that title and the responsibilities that go with it. Whether you sail with friends, family, or with your partner, before boarding the boat you should establish who will serve as skipper.

Other people aboard are either crew or passengers. Crew help to operate the boat. Passengers are simply along for the ride, but even they must be prepared to follow direction from both skipper and crew.

On a daysail, the skipper might assign jobs according to a crewmember's experience, ability, or desire to learn. That individual then "owns" that job, which might be steering, tending the jibsheets, trimming the mainsail, or acting as lookout, and must pay attention to his responsibilities until the skipper reassigns it.

TIP *A skipper need not ever drive the boat. The role of helmsman can be performed by any crewmember and even rotated around for fun. But the skipper's role remains attached to one person for the entire sail.*

Ultimate responsibility for the safe conduct of the boat rests with the skipper. He has to make decisions based on his knowledge and experience and the crew must be prepared to follow his instructions. A skipper who takes the trouble to describe a situation and explain the reasons for the orders he issues will have no difficulty finding willing and eager shipmates.

COMMUNICATION ON BOARD

To ensure everything aboard goes smoothly, communication must be clear and efficient. When information or an instruction is provided by either skipper or crew, the recipient should acknowledge it to ensure that he has received and understood the message. An effective way is for the recipient to repeat the information:

CREW: "Skipper, you have a blue powerboat off the starboard bow."
SKIPPER: "I see the blue boat off the starboard bow. Thank you!"

A positive response encourages further input, and kids especially will welcome the recognition that they are taking an active part in operating the boat.

For clarity in onboard communications, use the language of sailing, which over centuries has developed specialized terms to describe important objects, actions, and ideas. For example, the term "sheet" is specific where "line" is general. When you use standard nautical terms and commands, you will be better understood on any boat, and that makes a big contribution to both safety and team spirit aboard.

ISSUING AND ACKNOWLEDGING INSTRUCTIONS

1 **Skipper**	Preparatory Command, "Stand by!"	Alerts crew to prepare for a maneuver.
2 **Crew**	Acknowledgement	Message understood. Begins preparations, followed by, "Ready."
3 **Skipper**	Execute Command	Issues instruction to commence the maneuver.
4 **Crew**	Acknowledgement	Message understood. Takes required actions.
5 **Skipper**	Follow-up Command	Announces next successive action.
6 **Crew**	Acknowledgement	Message understood. Takes required actions.
7 **Crew**	Closing Reply	Action complete; standing by for the next command.
8 **Skipper**	Acknowledgement, "Thank you"	Crew stands down to await next command.

Onboard procedures go smoothly when everyone understands the goals and what they need to do to accomplish them. Individual skippers may choose to be very formal or quite informal, but they should issue commands in a simple and logical sequence. The accompanying "quick reference" box, above, uses the more formal terms.

The example might apply to tacking, jibing, or many other onboard maneuvers such as changing course or trimming sails

that might require action on the part of several members of the crew.

Crews used to working together might modify or even short-cut these steps, but it's still crucial that the communication is clear and gets the job done.

Some procedures can be referred to by one of several terms or phrases. For example, to tell the crew to prepare to tack, the helmsman might say, "Prepare to tack," "Ready to come about," or "Ready about." To avoid confusion, pick one term and use it consistently.

No two days of sailing are the same, so it's hardly surprising that novice and old salt alike will come away from every day of sailing with new lessons learned. Some days, everything goes well, others, not so well. When a maneuver doesn't work out as expected, take the opportunity to figure out what went wrong and why. The difference between a crew that enjoys safe, fun sailing and one that gets into scrapes usually comes down to how well they work as a team and how skilled and communicative the skipper is.

Clarity is key to onboard communications. By using simple protocols and the language of sailing, even a crew of strangers will quickly become a close-knit unit capable of performing any maneuver smoothly and without misunderstandings.

TIP *We all like hearing our own name. When giving commands, use a person's name to ensure everyone on board knows who is being called. If the skipper or crew merely tells "somebody" to do something, nobody will take action.*

CHAPTER 5

Sailing drills build sailing skills

It's time to get back on the water and review the concepts that we have learned by doing some sailing drills. If you are in a class, your instructor may have you rotate positions, from helm to mainsheet to jibsheet. It's important to be able to perform all these roles as you learn to sail because they all interrelate. By practicing these drills on the mainsheet, you will become a better helmsman and vice versa. Then we'll bring the boat back to the dock — which can be an adventure in itself — and put the sails away.

SAILING DRILLS

You have practiced making smooth, precise tacks, and you know how to sail on, and trim the sails for, every point of sail. Now it's time to put all that knowledge to work and see how tacking and jibing and sailing on different points of sail can bring you to a destination. As in any sport, proficiency comes with practice, and practice often takes the form of drills in which you repeat a sequence of actions over and over.

FIGURE-EIGHT DRILL — TACKING

Sailing a figure eight is a challenging exercise, and it's fun at the same time. We'll do it first with tacks, and then go the other way and jibe at the outside loops.

For this exercise, you need to find, or set, a pair of *marks* (some sort of anchored buoy) that are at least one minute of sailing apart, usually about 12 boat lengths. It's important that the line between them be perpendicular to the wind direction, so that when sailing from one to the other you are on a beam reach. They should be clear of other boats so you can focus on the drill. If no suitable marks are available, create imaginary marks and use clear verbal commands to prepare your less imaginative team members.

While this figure-eight drill emphasizes tacking practice, it also reinforces sail-trim techniques — getting the boat sailing fast enough to tack smartly around the marks.

① Approach the marks on a steady port-tack beam reach to pass about one boat length downwind of mark #1. Maintain your course.
② When the farther mark (mark #2) is nearly abeam, head up smoothly to close-hauled and trim both sails accordingly.

TIP *Remember to communicate early and clearly, both as helmsman and crew, to ensure all maneuvers are performed smoothly with no surprises.*

③ Begin tacking, turning smoothly around mark #2.
④ Continue your smooth turn, bearing away on starboard tack until the boat is on a course heading about one boat length downwind of mark #1. Ease the sails as you bear away. Your point of sail will be between a beam reach and a broad reach on starboard tack. Trim for this course.

TIP *It's important that all turns are done smoothly, so the crew can keep up with the sail trim and their movements around the cockpit, but with intent, so that you don't sail a lot of extra distance.*

⑤ When you get to a spot that's one boat length directly downwind of mark #1, head up to a close-hauled course and trim accordingly.
⑥ Now tack around mark #1, and bear away on a port-tack course heading one boat length downwind of mark #2.

TIP *It's important that the marks are at least one minute of sailing apart, so the crew has time to get settled sailing on a straight course before tacking again.*

⑦ Repeat the process, sailing a figure-eight pattern around the marks and tacking around each of them.

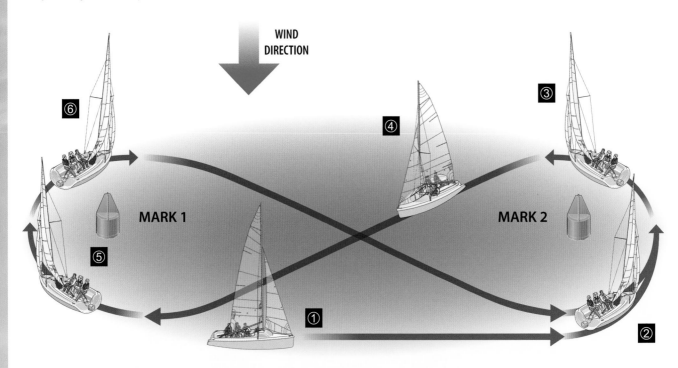

WIND
DIRECTION

MARK 1

MARK 2

FIGURE-EIGHT DRILL — JIBING

Precision and coordination between crewmembers are perhaps more important during a jibe than during a tack. If you flub a tack, you may lose a little headway, but if your team's timing is off in a jibe, the boom and mainsheet could cause problems as they sweep across the cockpit with great force. This figure-eight exercise will help you practice that coordination.

① Approach the marks on a steady port-tack beam reach to pass about one boat length upwind of mark #1. Maintain your course. When mark #2 is nearly abeam, prepare your crew to jibe.

② Begin bearing away and continue into a jibe as you sail around mark #2.

....

TIP *You should never whip off a rapid 180-degree jibe. Slow your turn enough when going through the actual jibe (broad reach on port tack to broad reach on starboard tack), so the mainsail can be jibed across safely and in control, and then accelerate your turn when the crew is ready to trim the sails.*

....

③ Set your course for a spot about one boat length upwind of mark #1. You will be sailing between a close reach and close-hauled on starboard tack. Trim for this course. Again, ensure that you have at least one minute of sailing before the next jibe.

④ When you get about one boat length directly upwind of mark #1, prepare your crew to jibe.

⑤ Bear away and jibe around the mark, performing all the necessary maneuvers with clear communication.

⑥ After the mainsail has been jibed safely, head up and aim for a point upwind of mark #2.

⑦ Repeat the process, following a figure-eight course as you jibe around the marks.

When doing these exercises, the goal is to get into a rhythm and maintain it for several consecutive laps. If you really botch a maneuver, take a break to get settled and discuss what went wrong. As you practice, you will find the entire crew anticipating each move and executing it with more and more confidence and fluidity. Switch positions and do more laps so everyone gets to do each job.

Sailing figure eights is a great way to perfect steering accuracy, crew communications, and maneuvering safely. Because you have to pay close attention to sail trim as the boat's course changes, you will quickly pick up the the knack of judging the wind's direction and the boat's angle relative to it. When you can perform these exercises correctly as helmsman and as crew, you can honestly begin calling yourself a sailor.

....

TIP *Since other boaters could be confused by your seemingly random maneuvers, be especially careful to keep out of their way. Never set up practice marks in a narrow channel or high-traffic area.*

....

By doing both figure-eight drills you will discover how much easier it is to do the tacking drill. In all but the lightest of breezes, tacks are easier for the team to perform than jibes, and you will be able to sail a much more accurate course with tighter turns around the marks. Because tacking is so much easier and controllable, in an emergency, and in strong winds, a prudent sailor always favors tacking over jibing.

In the jibing drill, the mainsheet crew is busy: Sheet in for the jibe, ease after it, trim for the reach, ease for the turn, and sheet in for the jibe again.

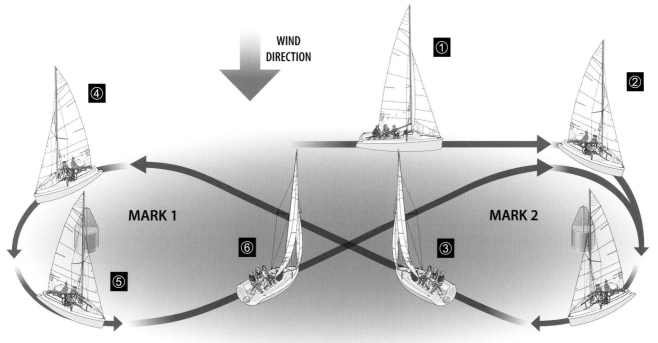

WIND
DIRECTION

④ ① ②

MARK 1   MARK 2

⑤ ⑥ ③

SLOWING THE BOAT UNDER SAIL

In your sailing exercises, you've been working hard to get the boat moving as fast as possible and to keep it moving during maneuvers. Sometimes, though, you may want to be able to slow the boat down, or even bring it to a halt. You certainly don't want to approach a dock at full speed, and you might want to slow and even stop the boat to retrieve a flyaway hat or, in the worst of instances, a person who's gone overboard. While learning, you've probably made a mistake or two, like getting stuck in irons, where the boat slowed down unintentionally. Now we will slow down intentionally, maintaining control while we do so.

WIND DIRECTION

SLOWING ON A REACH

This is an important drill to master: slowing the boat while under full sail and then, without losing steering control, accelerating again. This is a good trick since, as you slow down, the rudder loses its effectiveness. And when the boat is stopped, the rudder has no control over it at all.

① In an area clear of other boats, sail on a close reach. Pick an imaginary spot to stop. If possible, use a reference like a buoy and imagine your stopping point a few boat lengths downwind of it.

TIP *The first few times you try this exercise, you'll probably find the boat coasts faster and farther than you expect. Judge your boatspeed by watching the water moving past the hull.*

② Release the jibsheet, casting it completely off its winch or cleat. In stronger winds, the sail will flap violently, whipping the jibsheets. Take a little slack out of both sheets to quiet them. Try to find the maximum amount of sheet that you can pull in without trimming the sail, so it is still completely luffing and not driving the boat at all.

TIP *As you release the sheets to stop forward motion, the boat will heel less and the forces on the rudder will change. Adjust your steering so the boat maintains a steady, close-reaching course toward your imaginary target.*

③ Release enough of the mainsheet so the mainsail is completely luffing too. Now the heeling will be gone. With no driving force from the sails, the boat will really begin to decelerate. Hold that close-reaching course!

④ The boat will still keep moving through the water under its momentum until the frictional resistance of the water on the hull and *windage* (the frictional resistance of the wind on mast, flapping sails, crew, and boat) eventually bring it to a standstill.

MARKER

④

③

②

①

Bringing the boat to a stop at a predetermined location is a valuable skill to practice. It will come in useful when returning to the dock.

The boat will remain stationary for a few precious seconds before it begins to be blown downwind. In this drill we do not want to wait that long but will trim both sails at the same time to speed up again, and practice slowing and stopping again.

For the purposes of this drill, you do not actually want to stop the boat, because you will lose steering control. Instead, the drill is complete when the boat is still moving forward on a close reach at crawling speed — a very, very slow walk (less than 1 knot if the boat has a speedometer).

As you do this drill in a variety of conditions, you will learn how wind speed, waves, boat design, and sails will affect how far the boat will coast before stopping. The more you try it, the better you'll be able to predict the result. Once you are proficient at slowing the boat at

an imaginary point, find a mark (preferably a soft buoy) and try stopping the boat completely just a few feet downwind from it. This is a great trick to practice before attempting your first docking maneuver.

TIP Whenever possible, plan to slow the boat on a close reach (halfway between close hauled and a beam reach) because it is the most "forgiving" point of sail. Both sails can easily luff (which is not the case on a broad reach or run), and when you re-trim the sails just before the boat stops, the boat will move forward on the same course and the rudder will start working again (which is not the case if you are close-hauled or pointed directly into the wind). If you underestimate the distance that the boat will coast, you can trim the sails to get small burst forward.

TIP Never try to stop upwind (or up-current) of a mark, because with no steering control, the boat will be blown onto it.

SLOWING BY STEERING

As you've no doubt learned during your first sailing lesson, the helmsman can slow or stop the boat, without any help from the crew at all, by turning the boat toward the wind until it's stuck in the no-sail zone. Without any driving force, the boat will slow down, and if you do not turn back out of the no-sail zone, it will coast to a stop, and then be blown downwind with no steering control: in irons. Turning upwind is the fastest way to slow the boat, which can be useful in an emergency. But this method doesn't provide the same low-speed steering control as does slowing on a close reach.

When practicing stopping the boat at a mark, you will discover the point of sail below which the shrouds restrain the mainsail so it won't luff completely.

BACKWINDING THE JIB AND HEAVING-TO

When you set a sail *aback* (with the wind coming on the "wrong" side of the sail), it's called backwinding, or backing, the sail. Backing a jib can be helpful in two situations: to help the boat turn quickly, and to *heave-to* when the crew wants to take a break. You can also slow a sailboat down very quickly by turning into the wind and sailing against the backed jib for a few seconds before releasing it. By backwinding the mainsail, you can even sail a boat in reverse, but that is beyond the scope of our entry-level course.

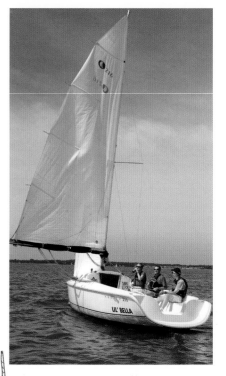

BACKING THE JIB IN A TACK

In light winds and on boats that are slow to tack, it's common practice to help the wind blow the bow through the no-sail zone by holding the jib aback for a few seconds. You do this by not immediately releasing the working sheet when the boat turns head to wind. In a small keelboat, if you are at full speed when you commence a tacking maneuver, you will not need the extra turning help of a backed jib. But if you commence the tack slower than half speed, or are stuck in irons, backing the jib will help turn the bow away from the wind onto the new close-hauled course.

TIP *If you are going to back the jib during a tack, ensure that the working jibsheet has enough wraps on the winch to resist the pull when the jib fills aback. Once the bow is turning out of the no-sail zone, release the working jibsheet. Don't hold it too long, or the backed jib will overpower the rudder and push the bow off course.*

With the jib and rudder set in opposition and the mainsail in "neutral," a sailboat will lie quietly hove-to, making slow progress crabwise.

HEAVING-TO

On our small keelboat in light to moderate winds, heaving-to is a great way to take a break. In ocean storms it's an effective way to have the boat more or less fend for itself while traveling slowly, safely, and under control.

① Beginning on a close-hauled course, instruct the crew that you want to tack and heave-to.
② Commence a normal tack, with all the proper sequence of communication, but leave the working jibsheet cleated.
③ As the boat turns onto the new close-hauled heading, leave the jib backed and release the mainsheet — the boat will begin to slow.
④ Push the tiller all the way to leeward so the boat travels along very slowly on a close-reaching course. The backed jib will be counteracting the turning force of the rudder. Congratulations! You are hove-to, and will be sailing along at about a quarter of your normal sailing speed in comfort, with very little heel. Aside from

keeping the tiller pushed hard to leeward, so the rudder is trying to turn the boat toward the wind, the crew will be free to open sandwiches or have a quiet chat. Don't forget to keep a lookout. Legally, you are still under way.

TIP *How an individual boat heaves-to is a function of many factors; design, keel type, and relative sizes of jib and mainsail are just some of them. You might need some trim on the mainsail (in strong winds you certainly don't want it flapping), which will require some adjustment to the rudder position. Heaving-to is a good technique to practice on any boat.*

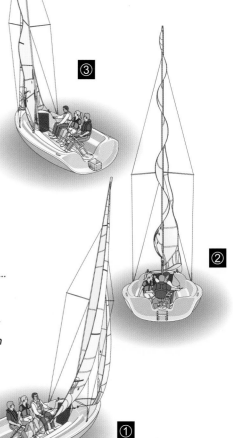

STOWING THE JIB

Just as the mainsail was the first sail to be hoisted, the jib is the first sail to be dropped. You may just want to reduce sail power if the wind has picked up, or simply give the crew a break. And coming in to the dock, the jib is rarely helpful in the final maneuvering under sail (and is often a distraction and impediment for the crew who want to be concentrating on handling dock lines). Here's how to get rid of that "front sail."

WIND
DIRECTION

DROPPING THE JIB
HEAD TO WIND

① Make preparations. Designate a crewmember who will uncoil the halyard tail and fake it so it can run out freely without tangles. Assign another to take a sail tie and move safely to the windward side of the foredeck, sitting or kneeling in a secure position.

② Turn the boat toward the wind, halfway between close hauled and head-to-wind on the present tack. Do not turn past head-to-wind or your foredeck crew will get hit with the foot of the jib and have an extra difficult job. Concurrently, pull any slack out of the leeward jibsheet

and keep some tension on the windward jibsheet to keep the foot of the jib above the foredeck. This technique will also calm the sail so it doesn't luff violently. (A flogging sail can damage itself and poses a risk of injury.) At this point of sail, the foredeck crew can work from the windward side of the jib, and won't need to lean overboard to recover it.

③ Immediately, release the halyard and let it run, so the sail drops as quickly as possible. Release the jibsheet so there is no more tension on it.

④ The foredeck crew gathers the sail onto the deck, pulling downward on the luff if necessary, and secures it with the

sail tie. He should also secure the halyard so the sail doesn't creep up the forestay.

⑤ Once the halyard is secure, the halyard crew takes out the slack, then coils and stows the excess line.

THE DOWNWIND OPTION

A main goal when dropping the jib is to make life as easy as possible for the foredeck crew to hang on and do his job. The sequence described above is the "traditional" way, and works well for a jib attached to the forestay with hanks, because the sail remains attached to the stay throughout the procedure and is easy to control.

Many sailors prefer to drop the jib, especially if its luff is in a luff foil, on a very broad reach. While the helmsman has to be on guard against the accidental jibe, the advantages of dropping a sail or performing any sort of foredeck work on this point of sail are many:

■ The boat is not heeling, so it's easier for the foredeck crew to move forward and hold on and do his job.

■ The jib will not flap violently but will just hang limp, hidden from the wind behind the eased mainsail, so it will be

easier to handle. Without the noisy flapping, skipper and crew can hear each other and communicate.

■ Dropping the jib while sailing downwind is easier on the boat and crew than doing so upwind, and it's always easier on any boat when sailing in stronger winds.

ROLLER FURLING

If your boat has a roller furler, there's no need for a crew on the halyard or foredeck. With the boat on an appropriate point of sail, such as a very broad reach, have one crew wrap the roller-furler line on a free winch, if one's available, and pull in on it while a second crew slowly releases the jibsheet so the sail is free of wind. As the sail rolls up on the stay, keep slight tension on the leeward jibsheet so the furl is tight and smooth. If the furl looks sloppy, ease off the furler line, pull the sail out with the

jibsheet, and then start again. Ultimately you want the entire jib to be wrapped around the forestay along with one or two full wraps of jibsheet for security. Cleat the roller-furler line and snug up the jibsheets to make everything tidy.

....
TIP *You should not need much of the winch's power to haul in on the furling line. If you do, it's likely something is caught somewhere. Stop winching and check the line, the sail, and the jibsheets for a possible hang-up.*
....

Once the jib has been dropped and secured on deck, it should usually be left there until the boat is docked. For safety, it's best to avoid jobs that require the crew working on the foredeck while the boat is under way. If it's calm enough, and you want to fold the jib while afloat, then you can follow the instructions at the end of this chapter.

SAILING THE BOAT TO A DOCK

Unless you've fallen so in love with sailing on your first day afloat that you've decided to head off to the South Pacific, you'll have to return to your dock or mooring. If your boat is moored in a crowded marina, your instructor may want to lower all sails and bring the boat in under power — in which case he will find another more open area to practice these crucial skills. Only a hundred years ago, the internal combustion engine was a novelty. Every sailor had to know how to sail up to and away from a dock. The best measure of your skills as a sailor will be how you handle a boat in close quarters. You've practiced slowing the boat in open water. Now it's time to use that technique to bring the boat into the dock under sail.

PLAN AHEAD

As you sail back toward home, note the wind direction and try to picture how it's blowing relative to the dock at which you hope to land. If you have a choice of landing spots, you're in luck, because some approaches are infinitely easier than others. As you draw near, assess the situation and put together a plan for maneuvering into the dock, and stopping the boat just as you reach it. Prepare well in advance for your landing, because to make it a smooth one, your team has to do several things quickly and well as soon as you reach the dock. For your first attempt, your instructor will choose a landing spot with a favorable orientation to the wind as described on the following pages.

DOCK LINES

First, you need to become familiar with some important equipment that you may have noticed when you set sail — *dock lines* and *fenders*.

When it's coiled and stowed, a dock line is a dock line. When being used to tie a boat into its berth, it has a specific name. Depending on the configuration of your dock and the direction and magnitude of the wind, waves, and current (and the rise and fall of the tide), a boat may need many dock lines to hold it secure. We'll cover how to secure the boat in detail in Chapter 7.

■ Bow line: the dock line that secures the bow. When the wind is blowing off the dock, a boat can be temporarily secured by this single line.

■ Stern line: the dock line that secures the stern.
■ Spring line: a dock line that keeps the boat from moving forward or aft. Springs can be secured in a variety of locations on the boat depending on the boat and docking configuration. For the purposes of our docking maneuver, we need a single spring line

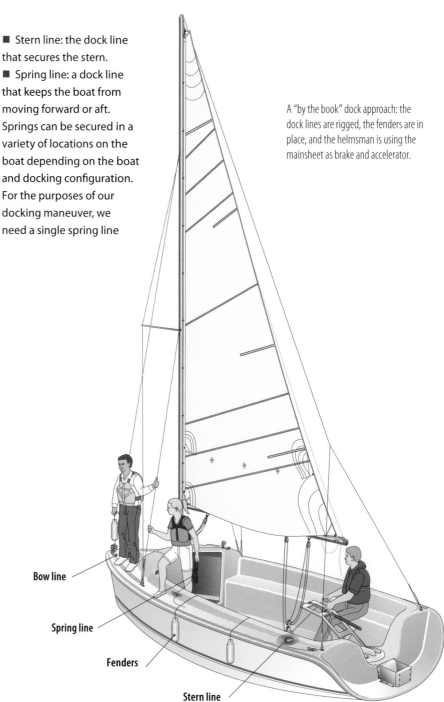

A "by the book" dock approach: the dock lines are rigged, the fenders are in place, and the helmsman is using the mainsheet as brake and accelerator.

Bow line

Spring line

Fenders

Stern line

When it's time to sail back to the dock, the wind doesn't always cooperate. The boat is approaching from downwind and the wind is blowing onto the dock (see page 84). Happily, sailing school staff are there to help.

attached to the side of the boat at its widest part and running aft to the dock. We will use this as a stopping spring to slow and stop the boat during the landing.

All dock lines must be attached to robust fixtures on both boat and dock. Most boats are fitted with dedicated cleats at the bow and stern for this purpose. To keep a dock line from rubbing on the hull of the boat, there may be a fixed metal fitting mounted near the cleat called a *chock* or *fairlead* through which the dock line will pass on its way to the dock or mooring.

FENDERS

Fenders protect the boat's hull from possible contact with the dock during the landing process and for as long as the boat is tied to it. When docking, you place them where they will lie between the hull and the dock.

Fenders come in many sizes and types, but those commonly found on sailboats are in the form of an inflated plastic cylinder with a line attached to one end. You will use this line, tied with the clove hitch or the round turn and two half hitches that were introduced in Chapter 4, to hang the fender from the lifelines or from some other convenient fitting.

Some docks are fitted with padding but it does not eliminate the need to hang fenders for "hard landings" and for long-term protection.

PREPARING FOR THE LANDING

Make sure the jib is secured and out of the way of the crewmember who will be working with the bow line.

If you are landing at an unfamiliar place, do a dry run. Take stock of the wind and current and also scan the dock to see which side of the boat will be alongside and to identify what you will be tying up to — cleats or pilings or rings — and how they are arranged. If you will be docking in a narrow slip, you may need lines and fenders on both sides of the boat.

Once you've determined which side of the boat will be alongside the dock, prepare your dock lines and fenders accordingly.

Attach the bow and stern lines to their cleats, lead them through their fairleads, if any, coil them, and set them down on the deck, ready for use. Make sure that when you pass them ashore, they will not become tangled with the lifelines (remember Murphy, the uninvited crew).

Attach the stopping spring line to the middle of the boat and lead it clear so

that a crewmember can step ashore with it, as it is a critical line to get onto the dock as quickly as is safely possible.

Tie a couple of fenders at the widest part of the boat hung at a level so they will protect the hull from the dock, but don't let them drag in the water — that looks sloppy. Keep an extra fender handy and assign a crew to be ready to drop it in a tactical place to protect the hull if needed.

Preparation is key. If you don't have dock lines and fenders ready for immediate deployment, a perfect landing can quickly deteriorate. The time to prepare is long before you come in on your final approach.

TIP *Docking under sail takes practice and knowing how your boat handles in a variety of conditions. If a procedure isn't going as expected, the wisest move often is to abort, sail into clear water, and try again. If you don't feel you can safely land at your chosen spot, find an alternative.*

TIP *Never, ever place any part of your body (like your hand) between the boat and any part of a dock or another boat. This rule applies to all boats, even lightweight dinghies. Let the boat suffer damage if need be. It can be repaired.*

DOCKING SAFELY

A boat that weighs hundreds, never mind thousands, of pounds has a lot of momentum even when it's moving very slowly. Regardless of your physical strength, you're no match for it. Never use any part of your body to attempt to stop a moving boat, even if it's on course for a hard landing. Your good intentions could result in severe injuries. That's where the crew with the roving fender can be worth his weight in gold — lowering the fender by its attached line to the perfect spot to protect the hull. If the boat is destined for a hard crunch, everyone else should back away from the point of impact and all crew should sit down or hold on to something solid to brace against being thrown forward when the boat stops abruptly.

DOCKING: THE IDEAL UPWIND APPROACH

In a perfect world, the wind would always be blowing parallel to the dock. You would approach your target from downwind, sailing in on a close reach so that you could employ the slowing and stopping skills that you practiced in open water. Your first docking practice should be at a dock aligned in such a way to the wind.

① Prepare for docking as described before: jib lowered and out of the way, fenders and docklines in place.

② Designate the crewmember who will step ashore from the middle of the boat with the stopping spring line.

③ Sail slowly toward a point one boat length downwind of your target on a close reach.

④ On the final approach, release the mainsheet completely to slow the boat. Err on the conservative side and begin slowing the boat a little sooner than you estimate necessary for the boat to just stop when you reach the dock. You can always put on a little more speed by re-trimming the mainsail for a few seconds at a time.

⑤ When you are a boat length or so downwind of the berth (you should be down to the pace of a very slow walk), turn directly into the wind. If you have judged perfectly, the boat will stop at your target.

⑥ As the boat comes next to the dock, have the crew with the spring line step onto the dock. This should always be done extremely carefully — no jumping! The shrouds can provide great support when disembarking. By wrapping the spring line once or twice around a cleat on the dock near the boat's transom and easing it, under control (much like easing a jibsheet on a winch), he can bring the boat to a gradual stop.

⑦ Immediately, another crew can carefully step onto the dock with the bow line and secure it to a cleat on the dock.

TIP *Attempting to bring a boat to an abrupt halt by simply cleating the spring line or by pulling on it, can cause damage or hurt you. Take a wrap with the spring line around the cleat or a piling but don't hold it fast — ease it as you do a jibsheet off a winch. The friction between the sheet and the cleat (or piling) will absorb the boat's momentum and bring it to a gradual stop as you apply increasing tension. Be ready to add another wrap around the cleat or piling if the spring line is pulling too hard to safely hold. This technique, called snubbing or surging, is very handy in maneuvers like docking.*

⑧ Ideally, the first crew ashore with the spring line can also bring the stern line and secure it immediately after cleating the spring line. If not, throw the stern line to the dockside crew to make it fast. The boat is now temporarily secure and you can drop the mainsail and furl it so that it doesn't luff any longer than necessary. For more permanent docking, you may need to rearrange fenders and add more dock lines. See Chapter 7 for how to leave the boat tied up for long periods.

TIP *If the wind is light and you are stopping short of your target, push back and forth with the tiller so the rudder works like a fish's tail to keep the boat moving.*

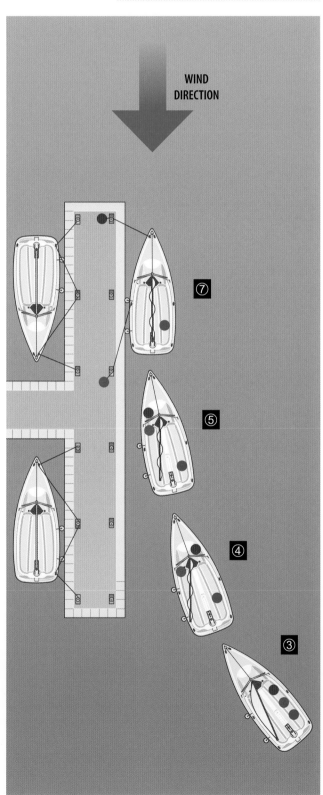

WIND DIRECTION

ANOTHER UPWIND APPROACH

When the wind is perpendicular to and blowing from the dock, you can still make the safe and controllable upwind approach, but there is less room for error. If you undershoot, you'll be blown back downwind, clear of the dock, and you can regroup for another attempt.

While making an actual landing is difficult, this condition presents a useful practice opportunity. If the dock is unobstructed, you can do "circuits and bumps" where you sail up to the dock, using the steps set out below, but instead of landing, you sheet in the mainsail and sail round for another approach.

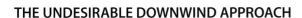

① Prepare the boat and crew for docking as described before.
② Make your approach on a close reach, slowing the boat and then controlling your approach speed with the mainsheet. Your goal is to reach the dock at a very slow walking pace.

③ When the bow is about to touch the dock, release the mainsheet fully and turn away from the wind, parallel to the dock, but close enough that the crewmember with the stopping spring line can step carefully onto the dock and wrap it on a cleat to slow the boat as

described above. If the boat is too far from the dock for the crew to safely get ashore, abort and try again.
④ When the boat comes to rest, the wind will blow it away from the dock, so secure the bow and stern dock lines as quickly as possible.

THE UNDESIRABLE DOWNWIND APPROACH

This maneuver, when the wind is blowing parallel with the dock and your approach is from upwind, should be avoided if at all possible. However, it should be part of your docking arsenal, just in case.

Traveling downwind with sails lowered, you have little control over the boat — and no way to stop the boat until you've made contact with the dock (hopefully with your fenders) and put a crew ashore with a spring line. You must bring the boat to a point upwind of your berth, luff up, drop the mainsail, and have enough residual speed that you can turn the boat 180 degrees to point downwind, then steer into your berth. The boat will come alongside the dock faster than in the upwind approach, and you can't stop it by luffing.

Practice dropping the mainsail first in open water. When you've got that down, practice this landing on a dock with an escape route farther downwind where you can rehoist the sails or put the engine in gear (that's not considered cheating!).

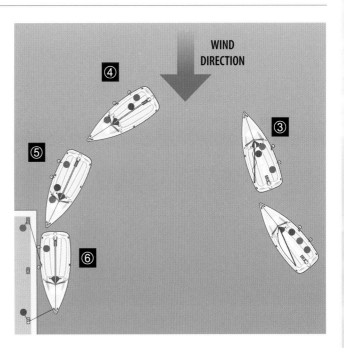

① Lower the jib, but leave the halyard and sheets attached if a possible downwind escape path is available.
② Prepare the crew, dock lines, and fenders as before.
③ Pick a point about five boat lengths upwind of your target. (Practice will teach you exactly where you need to be in what wind conditions.) Sail to that point, luff up, drop the mainsail, and quickly bundle it into a loose stow (explained

later in this chapter).
④ Before the boat loses speed and steering control, turn downwind and head for your berth. From this point on, you are committed and have no room for error.
⑤ As the boat draws alongside the berth, and it's safe to do so, have the spring-line crew step ashore from the middle of the boat, near the shrouds, to gradually slow and stop the boat in the manner described above.

⑥ Once the boat has stopped, quickly attach the bow and stern lines as before. Because too much speed can result in damage to the boat and possibly injury to crew, in certain conditions, such as strong winds, this docking approach would only be attempted in an emergency. In any event, in this maneuver it's a real help to have an extra crew roving with a fender to drop in place just before the boat hits the dock.

WIND BLOWING ONTO THE DOCK

A variation on the downwind approach occurs when the wind is blowing directly onto the dock. Again, because of the risk of damage, this maneuver should be avoided if at all possible. Here, if the dock is free of obstructions, your "stopping at a mark" exercise will pay off. Your goal is to stop the boat parallel with the dock and about half a boat length upwind and let the wind "park" you. You may have to drop the mainsail first, so keep the roving fender handy.

....

TIP *If the wind is very light, and there is no current, the danger of these downwind approaches is greatly reduced, making them a viable landing method.*

....

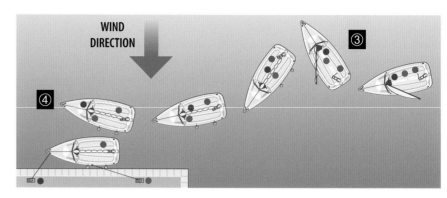

① Prepare the boat and crew for docking as before.

② If the wind is not quite perpendicular to the dock, approach from downwind if you can so you can slow the boat by letting the mainsail luff.

③ If the mainsheet and boom will hit objects on the dock, round up about five boat lengths from your target (the distance will depend on the wind and your boat speed), drop the sail, and coast in.

④ Aim to come to a stop about half a boat length upwind of your target berth. Once the boat stops, the wind will blow the bow toward the dock, so be ready with the fenders.

⑤ Stop the boat with the stopping spring and secure it as before.

Not all docking situations can be described as normal. Joining a raft-up like this (perhaps to listen to a concert) takes special care.

SAILING UP TO A MOORING

A great many boats don't have a permanent berth at a dock but are kept on *moorings* in a harbor. A mooring is a permanently anchored buoy to which a boat can be secured. Moorings are often used in harbors where docking space is limited. Boats are secured to the heavy mooring line or chain by a variety of arrangements. Your instructor will explain the specific system for your boat, most likely at the time you leave it in order to set sail. Depending on how the mooring is set up, you might need to ready the *boathook*, a long pole (sometimes telescopic) with a special hook at the end.

WIND DIRECTION

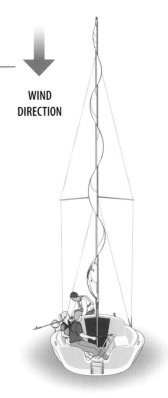

On a small boat with little room on the foredeck, it's sometimes easier to snag the mooring buoy from a little farther aft.

APPROACHING A MOORING

Being able to bring the boat to a stop within a boathook's reach of the mooring buoy is a valuable skill for which you practiced by performing the slowing drills. The approach is identical to the upwind dock approaches but, because there is no braking spring line to slow the boat, speed control is more critical. If you are too fast, you'll overshoot, and your crew won't have time to secure the boat. Too slow, and you'll stop short, get in irons, and have to get sailing again to make another pass. Just right, and the boat will sit head to wind long enough for the foredeck crew to secure the boat to the mooring.

① Drop the jib. Since tying to a mooring requires clear access to the front of the foredeck, you may want to stow the jib or move it and tie it down farther aft on the foredeck.

② Prepare a mooring line to use if the buoy arrangement requires it. It's prudent to have a line ready no matter what, as it may facilitate a quick temporary attachment to the mooring.

③ Have a crew stationed near the bow, holding onto the forestay for security, and ready with a boathook to grab the buoy or its mooring line.

④ Using your mainsheet speed control, approach slowly on a close reach toward a spot about three boat lengths downwind of the mooring buoy. You should aim to be traveling at a slow walking speed at this place. (The exact location of this spot will depend on the boat's momentum and the wind speed.)

⑤ When you reach this spot, release the mainsheet and turn directly upwind toward the buoy so the boat comes to a stop just as the bow reaches the buoy.

⑥ This is the critical point and swift action on the foredeck is key. Depending on wind speed, the boat will only be stopped for a few seconds. In these few seconds, the foredeck crew must swiftly grab the mooring line or buoy, using the boathook if needed, and secure the boat.

....

TIP *Don't try to be superman on the foredeck. If the boat is traveling too fast or if you can't get the mooring secured in time, simply let go of the mooring and smile at the helmsman. If the mooring buoy has been overshot, so you have hold of it at midships or back aft, don't wrestle it forward. Let go and let the helmsman try again.*

....

Don't be upset if you miss spearing the buoy, or don't get things secured before the force of the wind pushes the boat backwards out of reach. It's happened to everyone. Your mainsail is still up and you can easily make another approach.

⑦ Once the boat is secure, lower and furl the mainsail and secure the rest of the boat.

If at first you don't succeed, call it a practice run and go around again. With enough practice, you'll become adept at judging the stopping distance in a variety of wind conditions. In time, you'll be able to pick up a mooring on your first try every time, which is especially gratifying if you're performing before a crowd looking on from on shore.

....

TIP *If you have to tie your mooring line to a ring on the buoy, you can use a bowline, but the best way is with a round turn and two half hitches (see page 66). The round turn minimizes the likelihood of chafe. If you don't trust yourself to tie that hitch quickly, simply pass the end of the line through the ring, bring it back aboard, and attach it to the cleat.*

....

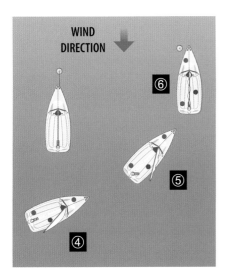

WIND DIRECTION

⑥
⑤
④

WHEN THE SAIL IS OVER

When your sail ends, you have to drop the mainsail and stow it properly. You might do this when you return to the dock, after you've picked up your mooring, or, if the boat has a motor, before docking. The procedure involves many of the same steps followed when raising it, only in the reverse order.

DROPPING THE MAINSAIL

① Prepare in advance. Assign a crewmember to the halyard, the mainsheet, the boom topping lift (if rigged), the boom vang, and to pull the luff down — doubling up tasks as needed.
② Retrieve the sail ties from their stowage while the halyard crew fakes out the coiled main-halyard tail so it can run freely. Make sure the bitter end of the halyard is either secured or has a stopper knot in it. The boom topping lift should be pulled hand-tight and securely cleated so the boom does not drop down when the mainsail is lowered.
③ When dropping the sail under way, turn the boat toward the wind, into the no-sail zone, stopping the turn about 5 degrees before being pointed directly into the wind. This allows the crew more space to pull down on the mainsail from the old windward side of the mast and boom.
④ Uncleat the main halyard, ease it slowly for a few feet, and then release the halyard completely so the sail can fall freely. If it's slow to come down, the crew at the mast must pull down on the luff. If the mainsail luff has a bolt-rope system, a growing amount of sailcloth will become free to blow around the deck. This may

require a crew up forward by the mast to keep the sail from blowing overboard or into the cockpit.
⑤ Once the sail is fully lowered, detach the main halyard and attach its shackle to its stowage point, normally on the end of the boom or out at the deck edge. Only when the halyard is shackled in place, tension the halyard to remove slack, cleat it off, and coil and stow the tail.

STOWING THE MAINSAIL

Once the mainsail is down, you have to secure it tidily on the boom, or remove it completely depending on the boat and the preference of the skipper. There are various systems for storing the mainsail on the boom that depend on the boat and the luff arrangement.

If the entire luff of the mainsail remains attached to the mast when stored, as with slugs or cars, then you will *flake* the mainsail as described below.
① To make a neat job, start at the mast by forcing the folds between the luff slides or cars so that they alternate to port and starboard.
② Go to the aft end of the boom and grab the leech about two feet from the clew on one side of the boom. Pull hard

and aft to force a crease parallel with the boom. While still holding this point, make a fold over the top of the boom, so that about one foot of the sail's leech lies on each side of the boom. Use your free hand or that of a crew to hold the first "fold" on the boom.
③ Continue the process, working up the leech two feet or so at a time making a series of folds that hang evenly on each side of the boom. Pull the sail aft before making the fold and hold the folded sail in place so it doesn't fall off the boom.
④ After you've made a few folds, wrap and tie a sail tie around them.
⑤ Continue until you have worked your way forward along the boom to the sail's head. Adjust each sail tie — normally there will be three or four of them spaced evenly along the boom — so that the sail is secure on the boom but not so tight as to permanently crease the sailcloth.
⑥ If available, fit the sail cover over the mainsail to keep it clean and protect it from damage.
If the luff is free of the mast, as with a bolt-rope arrangement, you can fold the mainsail in a similar way but with a crewmember pulling forward on the luff at the forward end of the boom.

When two crew flake the mainsail on the boom, one works from aft making the folds while the other tugs the sailcloth back toward him.

CARE AND HANDLING OF SAILS

Most mainsails and jibs are made of Dacron polyester, a durable and strong fiber that if treated properly will last a long time. No sail likes excessive flapping, so you should always limit luffing while sailing and always drop a sail when tied to a dock. Sailcloth is susceptible to damage by ultraviolet light, and excessive exposure to sunshine will reduce its useful life. Storing sails properly, or covering them when not sailing, will greatly extend their life. Never leave a sail exposed to the elements for long periods of time when it's not in use, either cover it or fold it and store it below deck.

When the mainsail is furled on the boom, a sail cover protects it from damaging sunlight and from rain, which can collect in the folds of the sailcloth and cause mold.

PROTECTIVE COVERS

The mainsail cover shields the mainsail from the damaging effects of the sun's ultraviolet rays while it's flaked and stowed on the boom. A jib on a roller furler stays hoisted all season. It's often protected by heavier sunscreen fabric strips that run the length of the leech and foot. When the sail is furled, these protective strips shield the Dacron sailcloth from exposure to sunlight.

FOLDING YOUR SAILS

If the sail will be stored belowdecks, then you must first fold it so it takes up less space and to avoid excessive creasing — never randomly stuff a sail into a bag or a storage bin.

The best way to fold a sail is by flaking it, as you did with the mainsail, because it's then ready for the next time you want to hoist it. If necessary, you can fold a sail on the boat's deck by laying it as flat as possible across the foredeck or side deck. It's much easier, though, to fold it on the dock once the boat is secured. Of course, the ultimate spot to fold a sail is a wide open lawn where you can first spread it out completely, but usually, if the boat is tied alongside a dock, it's easiest to flake it from the boat right onto the dock. This is at least a two-person job and will be easier with even more hands.

On many boats, the mainsail stays on the boom under a sail cover, so we'll focus on folding the jib.
① Unhank the luff from the forestay and detach the tack. Untie the sheets from

the clew and coil them neatly.
② Find the clew and tack, and hand each corner to a crew on the dock. If the dock is dirty, put a sailbag or something down to keep the sail clean.
③ Position one crew at the tack and one at the clew with the foot stretched taut between them. They should be kneeling, ready to begin folding. A third crew can be on deck preparing to feed the sail smoothly down to the dock as the folding progresses.
④ Grabbing the luff and leech about two feet up from their respective corners, the two folders pull firmly against each other to create a crease parallel to the foot and make the first fold. The size of

the folds will depend on the size of the sail — and the size of the sail bag.
⑤ While holding the first fold in place with one hand, the folders continue by moving up another two feet and repeating the process, trying to make the folded sail smooth and wrinkle free.
⑥ Once it's fully flaked, fold the sail lengthwise three or four times, starting at the clew end so the tack will be on the outside, ready for the next use.
⑦ Place the sail in its sail bag and stow it belowdecks.

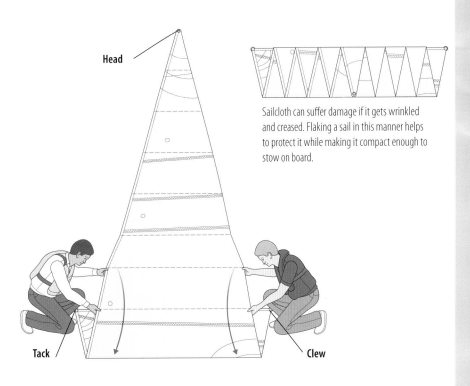

Head

Tack

Clew

Sailcloth can suffer damage if it gets wrinkled and creased. Flaking a sail in this manner helps to protect it while making it compact enough to stow on board.

REVIEW QUESTIONS (see page 126 for answers)

FILL IN THE BLANK OR MATCH THE LETTER WITH THE WORD

1 The fastest way to change the sail's power is to change its _____ to the _____ .

2 The shape of the mainsail may be changed by adjusting tension in the edges of the sail. Match the sail control with the edge of the sail it affects:

a Outhaul ☐ Luff

b Halyard or downhaul or Cunningham ☐ Leech

c Boom vang ☐ Foot

3 The outhaul changes the depth of the _____ of the mainsail.

4 Tightening the downhaul or Cunningham moves the draft of the mainsail _____ .

5 Tightening the _____ _____ holds the boom down on a downwind point of sail.

6 To get full power and optimum use out of the mainsail, _____ it until it just starts to luff, then trim the mainsail in so it just stops _____ .

7 Two ways to change the sail's angle to the wind are:

a _____ or _____ the sail.

b _____ _____ or _____ _____ .

8 The tendency for the boat to head up toward the wind on its own is called _____ helm.

9 The tendency for the boat to bear away from the wind on its own is called _____ helm.

10 While sailing close-hauled, four ways to decrease the heel of the boat are:

a Move the crew to the _____ side of the boat.

b _____ _____ slightly, into the edge of the no-sail zone.

c _____ the main _____ .

d Move the _____ to leeward.

11 Reducing the size of a sail so that less area is exposed to the wind is called _____ .

12 Match the following knots and hitches to their primary purpose or usage:

a Bowline ☐ Tie two ends of a line together

b Figure 8 ☐ More secure tie-up to dock piling

c Square knot ☐ Form a non-slipping loop, tie jib sheets to clew of jib

d Cleat hitch ☐ Keep line from slipping through a fairlead or block

e Clove hitch ☐ Secure a dock line to a horn cleat

f Round turn and 2 half hitches ☐ Temporary tie-up to dock piling, attach fenders to stanchion

13 When you want a break while sailing, you can make the boat lie _____ - _____ .

14 You heave-to by backing the _____ , easing the _____ , and putting the _____ to leeward.

15 Name the dock line used for each purpose:

a _____ _____ Secures the bow of the boat to the dock.

b _____ _____ Secures the stern of the boat to the dock.

c _____ _____ Keeps the boat from moving aft.

d _____ _____ Keeps the boat from moving forward.

16 _____ are used to protect the hull from contact with the dock or other boats.

17 The ideal point of sail on which to approach a mooring ball is on a _____ _____ .

18 Which of the illustrations shows the best conditions under which to approach a dock under sail?

☐ a ☐ b ☐ c ☐ d

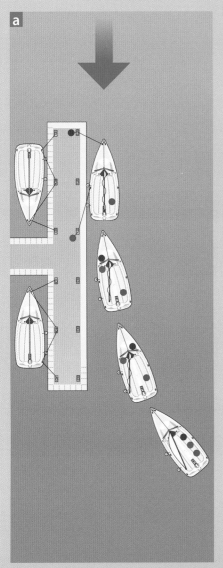

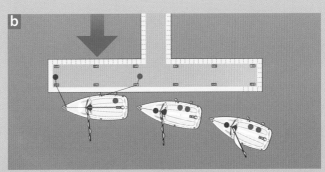

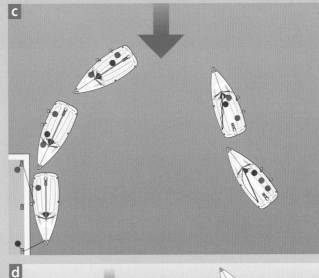

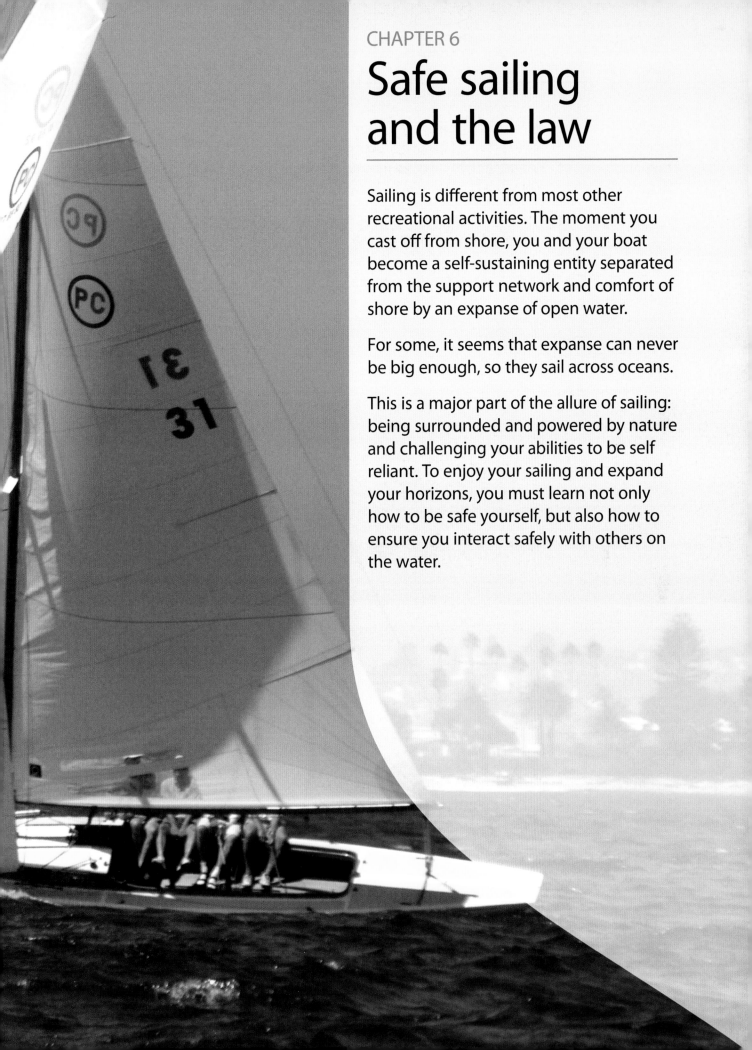

CHAPTER 6

Safe sailing and the law

Sailing is different from most other recreational activities. The moment you cast off from shore, you and your boat become a self-sustaining entity separated from the support network and comfort of shore by an expanse of open water.

For some, it seems that expanse can never be big enough, so they sail across oceans.

This is a major part of the allure of sailing: being surrounded and powered by nature and challenging your abilities to be self reliant. To enjoy your sailing and expand your horizons, you must learn not only how to be safe yourself, but also how to ensure you interact safely with others on the water.

SOME BASIC RULES TO LIVE BY

Untold numbers of vessels ply the world's oceans and waterways but a few simple rules govern their actions wherever their paths may cross. The rules that apply on the high seas are the International Regulations for the Prevention of Collisions at Sea, often abbreviated to "72 COLREGS." They are published in the United States Department of Homeland Security publication, *Navigation Rules*, alongside the Inland Rules that apply to U.S. Inland Waters.

ONE SET OF RULES FOR ALL

A driving instructor might advise students, "Drive for everyone else on the road." In other words, watch other drivers, anticipate their actions, and drive with enough caution to make up for the poor driving skills of others. On the water, boats of all types move in all directions and at different speeds, with no roads to guide them. Where buoys and other aids to navigation exist, they tend to shepherd all those boats into closer quarters, elevating the potential for collision. All this apparently random activity is brought to predictable order by the Navigation Rules, which apply to every vessel afloat.

While commercial vessels are operated by professionals who should be fully cognizant of the Navigation Rules and who, you hope, are diligent in observing them, recreational craft are usually in the hands of amateurs who might not know the rules or be as attentive as they should. When you factor into this mix the great diversity of vessels on the water operating at different speeds and with varying degrees of maneuverability, it's easy to comprehend why vigilance is required to avoid close encounters.

Always operate your boat with the same diligence you would expect of professionals, and keep a sharp lookout at all times — it's the law.

THE LOOKOUT RULE

The Navigation Rules apply equally to every vessel on the water. While they differ slightly in inland waters from international waters, and even to some degree under local jurisdictions, there is one that applies everywhere and you can begin observing it on your very first sail.

Rule 5: The Lookout Rule

"Every vessel shall at all times maintain a proper lookout by sight and hearing as well as by all means available appropriate in the prevailing circumstances and conditions so as to make a full appraisal of the situation and of the risk of collision."

Under this rule, every skipper has an obligation to be aware of what is going on all around the boat at all times. If, in the event of an accident, the authorities determine that Rule 5 was not followed (due to an absence of crew on deck, inattention to surroundings or prevailing conditions, or distractions), that vessel could be found wholly at fault and legally responsible for all losses and damages.

Rule 5 also refers to "sight and hearing." That means that as well as looking out for other vessels and hazards, the helmsman and crew should also listen for sound signals and voice hails from other boats. So, while a little music can add to the pleasure of sailing, be aware that too much volume can create a dangerous distraction.

Certainly, the skipper in charge bears the responsibility for maintaining a proper lookout, but in reality, all crew on deck share in the duty. Every crewmember can contribute by watching for and pointing out other vessels or potential hazards to the helmsman. For example, by calling out, "On the starboard bow, small blue sailboat approaching, about 100 yards away," you immediately direct the helmsman's gaze in the right direction,

In busy harbors, the Navigation Rules, when observed, bring order to potential chaos, but courtesy and communication are also invaluable.

and tell him what to look for.

Begin observing Rule 5 early in your sailing education and it will soon become what it should be — second nature.

WATCHING OTHER CRAFT

According to the Navigation Rules, whenever the possibility exists of a collision between two vessels, one is the *stand-on* vessel and the other is the *give-way* vessel. The stand-on vessel must maintain its course and speed and the give-way vessel must maneuver in a safe and seamanlike way so as to avoid collision. It is your job as skipper to determine whether your vessel is the stand-on or give-way vessel when encountering other vessels.

When several vessels are in the area, assess which one will make the closest approach soonest, and consider it first. For example, a vessel 100 yards from you and traveling in about the same direction and at a similar speed may be physically closer to you, but one that's 200 yards ahead and coming toward you presents the more immediate problem. Mentally pair your boat with this approaching one and establish which of you is the stand-on vessel. If you are the give-way vessel, take appropriate action immediately. At the same time, determine whether and how those maneuvers might affect your situation relative to other boats in the area.

When you are the give-way vessel, avoiding a collision will usually entail changing course. Do it early, and make the change bold enough that the other vessel's operator has absolutely no doubt that you are giving way.

Above all, avoid a collision. All vessels are expected to operate in a prudent and seamanlike manner and at all times at a safe speed for the prevailing conditions. When it comes to the imminent danger of a collision, everyone is responsible for doing whatever is necessary to avoid a collision, even the stand-on vessel.

All the above underlines the importance of maintaining a proper lookout at all times so you can assess collision risks in sufficient time to take the right action — even if the only action required is to maintain your course and speed.

LEGAL LANGUAGE

Note that all of a sudden we're using the term "vessel." This is because it's the term used in the Navigation Rules and it encompasses everything afloat, from a kayak or PWC to an aircraft carrier. All skippers of all vessels bear equal responsibility under the rules, regardless of size or armament. The first rule, though, is to be prudent.

HIERARCHY OF PRIVILEGE

While the Navigation Rules no longer use the word "privileged" to describe the stand-on vessel, the concept is still useful. The Rules recognize that a vessel which has great difficulty maneuvering should be given privilege over vessels that can maneuver more easily to stay out of its way. *Coastal Cruising Made Easy* looks at this "hierarchy" in more detail. For the present, and while sailing a small boat generally, you will be safe if you follow the rules discussed in this chapter.

....

TIP *The Navigation Rules as written are consistent in their intent: If the other vessel would find it difficult or impossible to get out of your way, don't expect it to!*

....

POWER-DRIVEN VESSELS

Under Rule 18 of the Navigation Rules, a power-driven vessel must give way to a sailboat under sail. This does not mean that when you are on a sailboat you can blithely assume every vessel driven by a motor will get out of your way. If, as is likely, you are sailing in a harbor, the issue of maneuverability may come into play. A large vessel is often restricted by its draft to navigating in narrow channels. In such a situation, a sailing vessel not similarly restricted — a small keelboat for example — becomes the give-way vessel.

....

TIP *A sailboat with its auxiliary engine running and in gear is considered a power-driven vessel. As such, it must obey the rules as they apply to a power-driven vessel, not a sailing vessel.*

....

TIP *While it's important to know the Navigation Rules, judging stand-on and give-way situations takes experience. Prudent sailors in small boats always keep in mind the "rule of tonnage" and stay well clear of larger vessels. Unlike nimble sailboats, big ships need time and lots of room in which to make a course change.*

....

In waters where large vessels may be restricted by draft to marked channels, sailboats must give them a wide berth. Participation in a race confers no special privileges.

CONVERGING COURSES

In any situation where two vessels are, or might be, on converging courses, their skippers must first evaluate where they lie in the hierarchy. A vessel lower in the hierarchy — more maneuverable — must give way to one that's higher — less maneuverable. A fishing vessel with nets in the water, for example, is "restricted in her ability to maneuver." As a sailboat, you would be required to keep out of its way, and you would be prudent to give it a wide berth so as to avoid its gear.

When neither vessel is restricted in any way, the Rules establish which is the stand-on vessel and which the give-way vessel. A give-way vessel must take action early and show its obvious intent to keep clear of the stand-on vessel.

RULE 13: OVERTAKING

When one vessel is overtaking another, the overtaking vessel must keep out of the way of the vessel being overtaken. In fact, this is one of the few instances in which a power-driven vessel is not the give-way vessel with respect to a sailing vessel. A sailboat under sail must keep clear when overtaking a power-driven vessel.

A vessel is considered to be overtaking you if it is approaching within an arc between your stern and 22.5 degrees aft of your beam on either side.

TIP *You can approximate the arc of the overtaking zone by facing the bow, holding your arms straight out, then pushing them back as far as you can. This gives you a practical way to assess whether an approaching vessel might be overtaking you.*

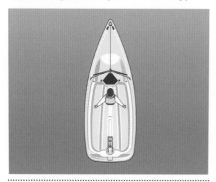

RULE 12: SAILING VESSELS

Sailing vessels have their own subset of rules which apply when the situation is not one of overtaking and the relative maneuverability of the vessels is not an issue. (You won't encounter many sailing vessels engaged in commercial fishing these days, but when you do, keep clear.)

When two sailing vessels are converging on opposite tacks, the vessel on starboard tack (with the wind blowing onto its starboard side) is the stand-on vessel and that on port tack is the give-way vessel.

In this instance, the port-tack sailboat should either turn, maybe even tack or jibe, or slow down to keep well clear of the starboard tacker. As in all situations governed by these Rules, make your maneuver early so the stand-on vessel understands your intentions.

Under this Rule, the position of the main boom determines a sailboat's present tack. If the boom is to starboard, the boat is on port tack, and vice versa.

TIP *Never attempt to sail across the bow of the stand-on vessel if there's the least chance you will pass close to it.*

When two sailboats on the same tack are approaching one another, the boat to windward is the give-way vessel. If a sailboat on port tack sights another sailboat approaching from windward and cannot determine the approaching vessel's tack, it should keep clear.

The windward boat would most often alter course to pass astern of the stand-on vessel. Again, make your move early and your intentions clear.

Remember, the overtaking rule applies before the sail-on-sail rules. And as soon as you turn on the engine and put it in gear, a sailboat becomes a power-driven vessel, and subject to the rules that apply to power-driven vessels. The wind is no longer a factor and the rules governing port-starboard and windward-leeward encounters don't apply.

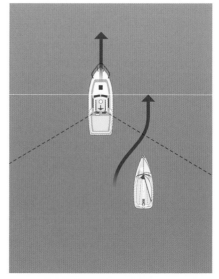

OVERTAKING VESSEL

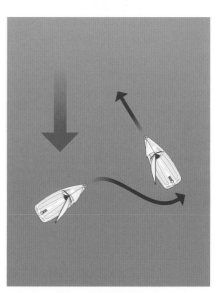

PORT TACK/STARBOARD TACK

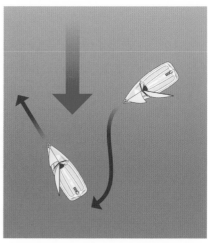

LEEWARD/WINDWARD SAME TACK

SOME BASIC RULES TO LIVE BY   95

Safe sailing and the law

RULE 14: HEAD-ON SITUATION

A *head-on* situation is one in which two power-driven vessels are *meeting* on virtually reciprocal courses. In such a situation, the Rules require both vessels to turn to starboard, so that they pass port side to port side.

TIP *In a narrow channel, this means that traffic keeps to the right side of the channel, and is described specifically in Rule 9: Narrow Channels.*

RULE 15: CROSSING SITUATION

If two power-driven vessels are neither meeting nor in an overtaking situation, they are, by definition, *crossing*.

When two power-driven vessels are crossing, the one that has the other vessel on its starboard side gives way. This rule is elegant in its simplicity, because by definition, only one of these boats can be to starboard of the other. Remember, your sailboat becomes a "power-driven vessel" the moment you start your engine and put it in gear.

SELF-PROPELLED VESSELS

Self-propelled vessels are those driven by oars or paddles. Stay out of their way.

APPROPRIATE ACTION

Once you've determined your status as the stand-on or give-way vessel in a situation that presents a risk of collision, the Rules describe how to proceed.

RULE 16: ACTION BY GIVE-WAY VESSEL

Whenever you find your vesssel to be the give-way vessel, you must take "early and substantial action to keep well clear" of the stand-on vessel.

RULE 17: ACTION BY STAND-ON VESSEL

As the stand-on vessel, your primary responsibility is to maintain your course and speed, because to do otherwise could confuse the give-way vessel as to your intentions. However, if the give-way vessel doesn't appear to be responding appropriately, you may take action to avoid collision. If a collision would be inevitable if you took no action yourself, you must take action.

It's possible for a situation to arise in which the other vessel fails to fulfill its obligations, or in which a collision would still result even if both vessels followed the Rules. Such eventualities are anticipated by Rule 2, sometimes referred to as the "General Prudential Rule", which requires all vessels to take any action necessary to avoid collision even if such action entails a departure from the Rules.

Once you understand the Navigation Rules and put them into practice, the risk of collision is very small.

TIP *The Department of Homeland Security imposes security zones around vessels of the U.S. Navy and, in some areas, around large commercial vessels and vulnerable shore establishments. Check with your local U.S. Coast Guard District office for those which apply in your sailing waters. Always stay at least 500 feet away from any naval vessel.*

QUICK REFERENCE

When there is a risk of collision, no matter how slight, you have to be prepared to take appropriate action, and watch the other vessel for signs of actions it might be taking. Become familiar with this condensed list and you will be prepared for most situations you'll encounter on a day sail.

1	RESTRICTED MANEUVERABLE	Stands On Gives Way
2	OVERTAKEN OVERTAKING	Stands On Gives Way
3	SAIL ONLY POWER DRIVEN	Stands On Gives Way
4	STARBOARD TACK SAIL PORT TACK SAIL	Stands On Gives Way
5	LEEWARD SAIL WINDWARD SAIL (both on same tack)	Stands On Gives Way
6	HEAD-ON (power)	Turn to starboard, to pass port to port.

Select "textbook links" under the "sailing resources" section of www.asa.com for more on the Navigation Rules.

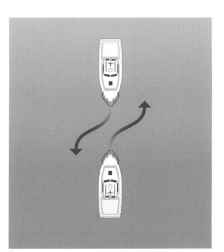

POWERBOATS MEETING

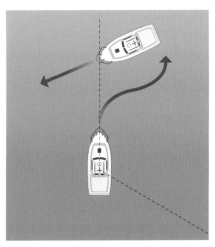

POWERBOATS CROSSING

BOATING AND THE GOVERNMENT

You have already seen that the Navigation Rules establish how vessels of different types and maneuverability can safely share the waterways. At the national and local level, further regulations help assure a high level of safety aboard recreational boats.

FEDERAL AND LOCAL REGULATIONS

At the national level in the U.S., the federal government has enacted regulations intended to promote safety in recreational boating. These federal rules specify safety equipment that must be carried aboard vessels according to their size and use. Federal jurisdiction covers inland lakes and rivers as well as coastal waters and the high seas within the limits of U.S. waters. The United States Coast Guard (USCG) enforces these regulations.

In addition to the federal regulations, most states have supplementary laws and regulations. The USCG cooperates closely with state and local law enforcement authorities in enforcing all applicable regulations.

Newcomers to boating are often surprised at how lightly regulated the pastime is and how few specific requirements apply to smaller sailing vessels, especially those under 26 feet with no engines. Larger boats with engines and more complex systems are slightly more burdened, but the equipment required by law is no more (and usually less) than you would wish to have aboard anyway.

Under federal regulations, a license is not required to operate a pleasure craft. Individual states, however, are beginning to phase them in. Be sure to check the requirements that apply in your state.

REGISTRATION

Every state has its own requirements for registering boats. Generally, any boat with a motor has to be registered, must display its registration number on both sides of the bow, and must carry its registration aboard. Small sailboats are sometimes exempt. Check for the rules in your state. Larger vessels may be documented with the USCG Vessel Documentation Center.

ALCOHOL AND DRUGS

In the old days, sailors had a reputation for enthusiastic consumption of alcohol, and the raucousness that usually accompanies it. In fact, until 1970, Britain's Royal Navy issued sailors a daily ration of rum to ease the hardships of life at sea. Today, the practical and legal ramifications of over imbibing, require sailors to be more circumspect.

The skipper is responsible not only for the safe conduct of the vessel but also for the welfare of everyone aboard. Every member of the crew has a parallel duty to follow orders, keep a lookout, and conduct himself in a sober and responsible manner. The use of alcohol and drugs on board a vessel can have serious life-threatening consequences. The mere possession of illegal drugs can put the boat at risk of confiscation. In most states, operating a vessel under the influence of drugs or alcohol is treated and penalized exactly like driving a vehicle under the influence, and can result in revocation of the skipper's automobile license. Boating Under the Influence (BUI) at a Blood Alcohol Content (BAC) level of .08 percent or higher is currently a specific federal criminal offense (some states vary the BAC threshold slightly). Information on BUI and tips to avoid problems are posted on the Office of Boating Safety website (www.uscgboating.org).

A good skipper will set clear limits for the use of alcohol aboard the vessel. For many, this will mean no alcohol consumption until the vessel is back to shore or at anchor. Even then, the skipper should designate enough crew to competently handle the boat should the need arise. They are effectively the equivalent of designated drivers.

Boats that are required under state law to be registered must carry the registration number on the bow.

REQUIRED SAFETY EQUIPMENT

The United States Code of Federal Regulations (CFR) requires certain safety equipment be carried on board, the nature and quantity of which are largely determined by the vessel's size. Among the safety equipment with whose use you will need to become familiar early in your sailing career are life jackets, distress signals, fire extinguishers, and navigation lights.

Life jackets are required aboard all boats, and sensible sailors know when to wear them.

LIFE JACKETS

Life jackets save lives. A vessel under way must carry a USCG-approved life jacket for every person aboard. The jackets must be readily available for use and the correct size for the individual user.

In the official language of the USCG, a wearable device that will keep you afloat should you fall in the water is a "personal flotation device" or "PFD." PFDs are officially classed as Types I, II, III, IV, and V, according to their design, construction, and intended use. The specific type required aboard depends on the type of vessel, its use, and the waters in which it sails. Aboard our small keelboat, each person's life jacket must be Type I, II, or III. Any boat over 16 feet must, in addition, carry one Type IV throwable device.

The manufacturer's label on a PFD provides information about the PFD's type and its approval and weight ratings. Standard PFDs have a fabric shell into which a buoyant material is securely

stitched. Inflatable PFDs are a lightweight alternative to their foam-filled counterparts, but to qualify as part of a boat's required equipment, inflatable life jackets must be worn.

A life jacket in the manufacturer's packaging and stowed out of sight in the cabin has no lifesaving value in an emergency — and doesn't comply with the regulation that it be readily available. If the life jackets are not being worn, keep them in a designated and labeled stowage location in or close by the cockpit. Everyone aboard should know how to find, put on, and adjust their life jacket before setting sail.

Most state laws require that children under a certain age wear a life jacket when afloat. And it is just plain common sense that life jackets should always be worn on dinghies (which can capsize), on keelboats without lifelines, and by anyone on any boat who feels the slightest bit uncomfortable about not wearing one.

The skipper should encourage everyone aboard to wear a life jacket and, when necessary, require crewmembers to wear them. His decisions may be based on such factors as age, experience, or physical condition, whether the individual has to leave the cockpit to work on deck, the type of boat, and the weather conditions. Many skippers require every crew to wear a life jacket at all times on deck. When it comes to safety, more is always better.

PFD TYPE AND CHARACTERISTICS

Type I	**Offshore Life Jacket** Most Buoyant, WILL roll unconscious person face-up, used in rough water and required on commercial vessels.

Type II	**Near-Shore Buoyancy Vest** Foam vest MAY turn unconscious person face-up.

Type III	**Flotation Aid (Inland Use)** Intended for light use, presumes a conscious person. More comfortable than Type I. Examples: waterski vests, fishing vests, belt-pouch inflatables.

Type IV	**Throwable Device** Not designed to be worn. Thrown to victim in water to grasp until rescued. Examples are horseshoe buoys, life rings, and floating cushions.

Type V	**Special-Use Device** Hybrid devices such as hypothermia suits, work vests, commercial deck suits, and inflatable life vests.

VISUAL AND SOUND SIGNALS

If you have an emergency of any kind aboard your boat, you will want to attract the attention of nearby vessels. Prescribed devices for signaling distress include pyrotechnics, lights, horns, and bells.

Vessels that are required to carry visual signals have some choices. Pyrotechnic devices are available for use in daytime (smoke) and both day and night (flares). Alternatively, a vessel may carry an approved emergency flag for daytime use and an electric light that flashes SOS in Morse Code automatically for nighttime use. The devices and number of each needed to meet the requirement are shown in the table below.

Three handheld red flares, for example, will meet the requirement for both day and night signals, but three smoke signals meet only the requirement for daytime use and will have to be augmented by flares or the distress light.

Pyrotechnics are all marked with an expiration date past which they will no longer meet the legal requirement and must be replaced. They will likely still work, and there's no harm in keeping them aboard to supplement those with valid dates.

It is illegal to launch or display distress signals except during a genuine emergency at sea, and the U.S. Coast Guard will prosecute anyone who willfully disregards this law or utters false emergency calls by any means.

Federal law sets a minimum requirement for carrying fire extinguishers aboard vessels with enclosed compartments.

Vessels under 16 feet in length and open sailboats that are under 26 feet in length and not equipped with engines are not required to carry day signals. These vessels, however, must carry night signals if operating between sunset and sunrise.

SOUND SIGNALS

The Navigation Rules require vessels under 12 meters (39 feet 4 inches) in length to carry some means of making an efficient sound signal. Many recreational vessels comply by having on board, within easy reach of the helm, a handheld air

horn or an athletic whistle. Specific sound signals and their meanings are covered in *Coastal Cruising Made Easy*. The most important to know now is "five short whistle blasts." Commonly called the "danger signal," it is sounded by a vessel that is unsure of the intentions of another or is in doubt whether sufficient action is being taken to avoid a collision.

FIRE EXTINGUISHERS

Fire on a boat carries some consequences not experienced in a house or vehicle fire ashore. Jumping overboard is often not a prudent option, so you have no alternative but to put the fire out before it causes injury or significant damage.

Federal law requires firefighting equipment to be carried aboard any vessel where a fire hazard could be expected. Many small sailboats do not have motors or fuel on board, but simply having a closed compartment or closed living space might require you to carry a fire extinguisher.

Sailboats less than 26 feet in length that require firefighting equipment must have one USCG-approved Type B-I fire extinguisher that is in good condition with pressure in the proper range. Suitable devices are clearly marked "Marine-Type USCG" and are about the size of a quart of milk. Larger boats with more elaborate propulsion machinery require more extinguishers, larger sizes, and additional precautions. Sailboats from 26 feet up to

---

SIGNAL DEVICES (FOR DAY AND NIGHT)

Handheld Red Flares (3)
Similar to railroad flares.
Day or night

Red Aerial Flares (3)
Meteor flares from flare pistols or hand launchers.
Day or night

Orange Smoke Signals (3)
Some are handheld; some float in the water.
Day only

Distress Flag (1)
Orange 3 x 3-foot flag with black square and ball.
Day only

Electric Distress Light (1)
Special handheld white light that automatically flashes SOS in Morse Code.
Night only
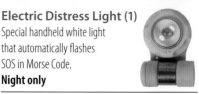

Air Horn
Used to send sound signals.
Day or Night

under 40 feet are required to carry two Type B-I fire extinguishers or one Type B-II extinguisher.

The designation "B-I" conveys critical information about the extinguisher: The type of combustible material it is designed to extinguish and the quantity of extinguishing material it contains. Type B extinguishers are certified for fighting petroleum-based fires, which includes burning fiberglass, but they can also be effective against other types of fires. The Roman numeral "I" indicates a small capacity. Get into the habit of checking the location and condition of every fire extinguisher on board.

NAVIGATION LIGHTS

Operating a boat without lights at night is both dangerous and against the law. The Navigation Rules describe a system of lights to be displayed by any vessel so that it can not only be seen from other vessels at night (or during reduced visibility) but also identified as to size and in what activity it's engaged. Further, an observer can determine from the lights visible on another vessel the relative direction in which it's headed.

At this stage in your sailing career, your sailing will be limited to the daylight hours. But just in case, you do need to know what lights are required on your boat and how to quickly determine whether you need to make allowances for other vessels displaying their lights.

All sailing vessels over 7 meters (23 feet) in length, when under sail alone must show a green *sidelight* on the starboard side, a red sidelight on the port side, and a white *stern light*. Each sidelight should be visible through a 112.5 degree arc, from the boat's bow to 22.5 degrees abaft the beam on its respective side. The stern light's 135-degree arc completes the circle. Anyone on another boat will see only one of your lights at any time except when they are dead ahead of you, when they will see both your red and your green sidelights.

You have already encountered these

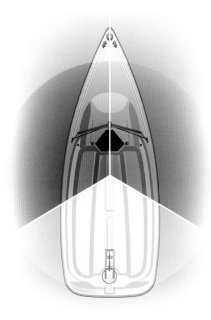

Navigation lights are required at night. From the colors visible, another boat can tell the direction it's moving.

arcs of visibility in the Navigational Rules where you learned to determine whether you are crossing, overtaking, or being overtaken by another vessel. At night, if a vessel is approaching you within the arc of your stern light, it is overtaking you. If it is approaching within the arc of your green, starboard-hand sidelight, it is the stand-on vessel.

Under the Rules, a sailing boat under 7 meters in length should carry the same lights as required on bigger boats "if practicable." If your boat is not so equipped, you must have a white light "ready to display to avoid a collision."

Shining a bright white light on your sails is a great way to draw attention to your boat regardless of whether your boat shows running lights.

Power-driven vessels (including sailboats under power) under 12 meters (39 feet 4 inches) in length must show the same red and green sidelights and a 360-degree white light. Sailboats with engines usually have a white *steaming light* mounted partway up the mast which shines in the 225-degree forward arc covered by the red and green sidelights combined. Together with a stern light that shines in a 135-degree aft facing arc, this steaming light completes the 360-degree white light required when under power. (Some sailboats have a white masthead light that shows in a full 360 degrees but this does not count.) Lights should always be displayed between sunset and sunrise and at times of reduced visibility, such as in fog.

When anchored at night, it's wise to display a 360-degree white light for safety. The Navigation Rules require anchored sailboats and powerboats over 7 meters (23 feet) in length to display this sort of anchor light unless anchored in a specially designated anchorage area. Sailboats under that length don't have to show an anchor light as long as they are clear of areas where other vessels might be operating.

In reduced visibility, all vessels that are required to carry navigation lights, and this one would qualify, must display them.

AIDS TO NAVIGATION

Finding your way around on shore is easy. You look at a map and then follow roads to get to your destination. It's quite obvious where the road is and where it isn't. It's very different navigating on the water — there are no roads but there are underwater hazards that could end your sail in a hurry. In most instances, a patch of water that's deep enough for your boat looks pretty much the same as one that's too shallow.

THE LATERAL SYSTEM OF BUOYAGE

In many areas the government deploys marks to indicate deeper-water channels and danger areas. These *aids to navigation* and the channels and dangers they mark appear on *navigational charts*. You will study charts later in your sailing career, and discover all the valuable information they contain.

Aids to navigation usually take the form of floating *buoys* anchored to the bottom or *beacons*, fixed structures positioned on land or in the water. A beacon often displays a *daymark* to make it clearly visible

Buoys and daymarks are designed and colored so that, even from a distance, mariners can distinguish them and determine their purpose.

Around the world, two separate but related systems are used for marking danger areas and defining the perimeter of a channel. All of North America employs the same "lateral" system of navigation aids, (IALA Region B). Supplementary types of marks are used in inland waters.

The left- and right-hand sides of a channel are distinguished by marks that differ in color, shape, and numbering.

REGULATORY MARKERS

Information and Regulatory Markers are white cylindrical buoys with orange stripes above and below one of four shapes.

A diamond shape warns of Danger at that location. A diamond shape with a cross inside indicates an Exclusion Zone (boats keep out).

A circle marks a Restricted Operations area, such as a speed-limit or no-wake zone.

A rectangle is used to display information such as directions or distances.

DANGER

RESTRICTED OPERATIONS

EXCLUSION

INFORMATION

COLOR

In IALA Region B, red marks indicate the right-hand side of a channel when you are returning from the sea or moving from a large body of water to a smaller body of water. The phrase "red, right, returning" will help you remember this system. Green marks indicate the left-hand side of a channel when you are returning from the sea. Some lateral marks also have corresponding red or green lights that flash in recognizable patterns to aid navigation at night.

SHAPE

Fixed marks and unlighted buoys on the edge of a channel have characteristic shapes. Fixed red day beacons are triangular, apex upward. Unlighted red buoys are cylinder-shaped, tapering at the top, hence the name *nun* buoys. Fixed green day beacons are square. Unlighted green buoys are shaped like a can and are called *can* buoys. Red and green lighted buoys are not necessarily differentiated by shape.

NUMBERING

Each channel mark has its own number, starting with marks 1 or 2 at the beginning of the channel when entering from the sea or a larger body of water.

The sailboat is motoring in the channel toward open water, so is leaving the red daymark to port and the green lighted beacon to starboard. Note also the white and orange Restricted Operations buoy.

Odd numbers identify the green, or left-hand, side of the channel (as you return from the "sea"), and even numbers identify the red side. Sometimes the sequence skips a number, and this will be evident on the chart. Navigating a marked channel is as simple as knowing which side of the marks you should be and staying there — in the deep-water channel.

TIP *With all this talk about "red, right, returning", remember that when you leave the harbor, the red buoys and beacons should be passed on the left side. In IALA Region A (most of the world outside North America) the lateral colors are reversed. Consult the Sailing Directions or local cruising guides when navigating overseas.*

SAFE-WATER BUOYS

Safe-water buoys have vertical red and white stripes and a ball at the top, or are round balls similarly striped. They are deployed in deep water where they can be safely approached from all sides and often mark the seaward approach to a channel or the center of a channel.

JUNCTION MARKS

A junction mark, also known as a "preferred channel mark," marks a fork in the channel. The color of a junction mark indicates the direction of the primary channel and a horizontal "waist band" indicates the direction of the secondary channel: A red junction mark with a green band marks the red side of the primary channel and the green side of the secondary channel. Safe-water marks and junction marks are not numbered but may have a letter for identification.

SPECIAL MARKS

A number of other marks are used to convey information and indicate hazards. Select "textbook links" under the "sailing resources" section of www.asa.com for more on buoys and navigation aids in the U.S.

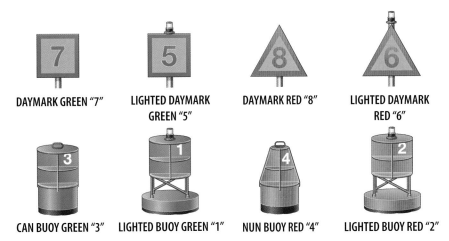

DAYMARK GREEN "7"   LIGHTED DAYMARK GREEN "5"   DAYMARK RED "8"   LIGHTED DAYMARK RED "6"

CAN BUOY GREEN "3"   LIGHTED BUOY GREEN "1"   NUN BUOY RED "4"   LIGHTED BUOY RED "2"

Colors, shapes, and numbers are used to identify and distinguish aids to navigation. In North American waters, red aids mark the starboard, or right-hand, side of a channel for vessels traveling inland or upstream from seaward.

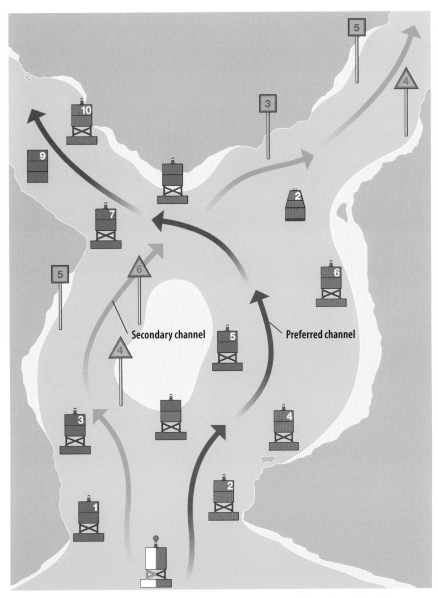

In the IALA Region B system of lateral buoyage used in North America, red buoys and daymarks mark the right- or starboard-hand side of a channel as it leads inland from the sea.

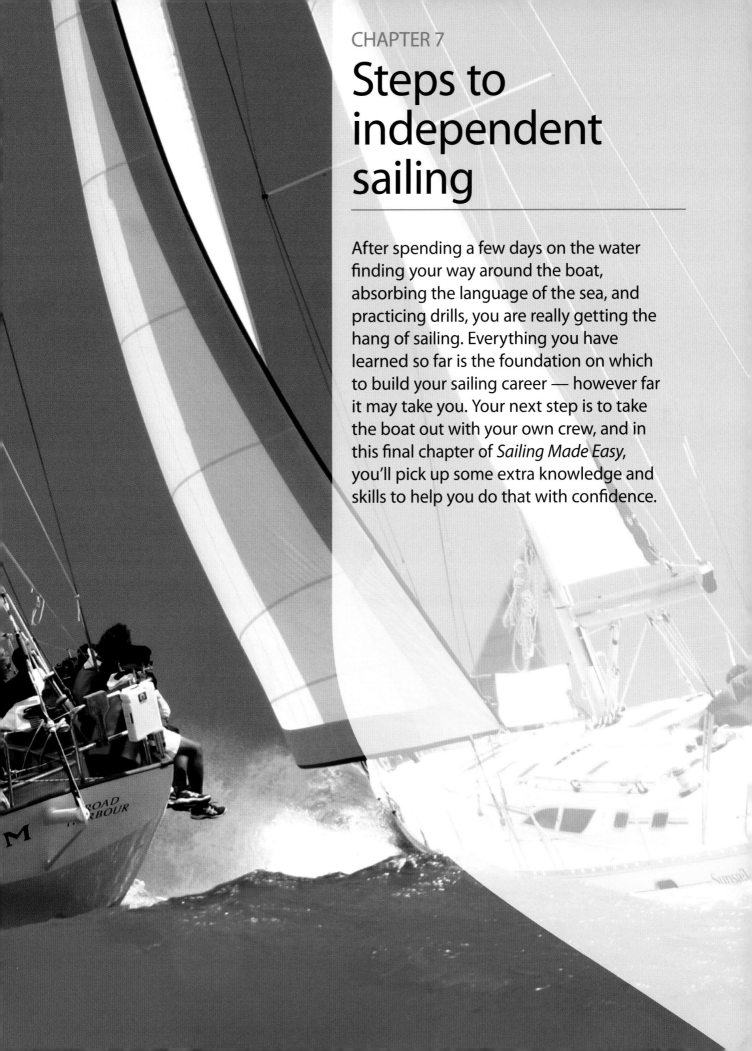

CHAPTER 7

Steps to independent sailing

After spending a few days on the water finding your way around the boat, absorbing the language of the sea, and practicing drills, you are really getting the hang of sailing. Everything you have learned so far is the foundation on which to build your sailing career — however far it may take you. Your next step is to take the boat out with your own crew, and in this final chapter of *Sailing Made Easy*, you'll pick up some extra knowledge and skills to help you do that with confidence.

SECURING THE BOAT IN ITS DOCK

When your day of sailing is over, you'll head home and immerse yourself in your usual routine and probably not think too much about the weather and what's going on in the marina where you left the boat. But wind and water never rest, and even on the calmest of nights, they will cause the boat to tug at its lines. That means once you've brought the boat safely into its berth, as covered in Chapter 5, you'll have to tie it securely so it can't swing around and damage itself or other boats.

DOCKING PLACES

How you secure the boat will depend on a number of factors, the most important of which is the type of berth it's in.

Docking is the process of bringing a boat into its berth and securing it there. You might *dock* your boat alongside a *quay* (a solid structure), a *pier* (a structure built on pilings), a *pontoon* or *floating dock* (secured to pilings but free to rise and fall with the tide), or in a *slip* (a space between finger piers or pilings). Any one of these places may be called a *dock*.

Each berth will be furnished with cleats, rings, or other fittings (sometimes simply the pilings) to which you secure the dock lines.

THE ALONGSIDE BERTH, OR SIDE TIE

When we docked the boat, we employed a single stopping spring line, a bow line, and a stern line. Now we will re-rig and add to our web of dock lines and fenders so the boat remains safely in the desired position alongside a floating dock.

For our side tie alongside the quay, pier, or pontoon, we will employ two spring lines: the aft spring line, which we

used to stop the boat, and a forward spring line, led from the middle of the boat forward. They should be long enough so that when secured to the dock, they are at about a 15-degree angle to the centerline of the boat. Once adjusted, these spring lines should be relatively taut as they keep the boat in position at the dock. The bow and stern lines should lead forward and aft respectively at about a 45-degree angle to the dock from their attachment points on the boat. Don't make these too taut. Ideally, the boat will float parallel to the dock and just off it, so it doesn't rub.

Once the dock lines are set, check your fenders. Adjust them as needed to ensure they are positioned evenly on either side of the hull where it's closest to the dock. They should be well secured and hanging where they fully protect the hull from the dock and low enough that they can't work their way up and out of position if the boat moves in waves.

Make sure your dock lines are amply strong and thick. For a 25-foot keelboat, the line used should be at least 7/16-inch diameter. Nylon line is favored because its inherent elasticity absorbs shocks.

GUARD AGAINST CHAFE

Constant movement resulting from waves and tidal action can cause the dock lines to wear against anything they touch. Over time, the resulting *chafe* can wear all the way through even the toughest dock line. If the boat will be tied up for a long time or in rough conditions, fit some sort of *chafing gear* to protect the dock lines. Heavy canvas, a section of garden hose, leather, or in a pinch, rags from your old jeans wrapped around the line at the point of wear can save the line and, where the boat has no chocks, chafe damage to the boat itself.

TIDE CONSIDERATIONS

A boat tied to a quay or fixed pier will rise and fall with the tide. If the tidal range is large, you may have to adjust the lengths of the lines and reposition the fenders frequently. The boat will handle the tidal changes with less-frequent tending if you extend and secure your dock lines, especially the spring lines, farther forward and aft on the pier than you would in a location where there is little or no tidal range. When you moor a boat to a floating pier, the boat and dock move together with the tide, so the dock lines, as long as they are tied to the pier and not to its fixed pilings, don't need to be adjusted as the tide changes.

Floating docks are common in tidal waters.

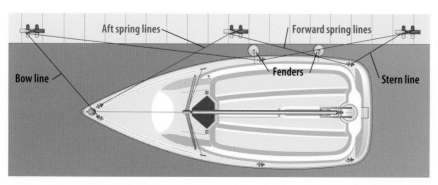

Aft spring lines   Forward spring lines

Bow line   Fenders   Stern line

A bow line, a stern line, one forward spring (shown in red), and one aft spring (shown in green) usually suffice to secure a boat in a side tie. The locations of fittings on the dock and on the boat may affect the choice of spring lines used.

ANCHORS AND ANCHORING

Of all the seamanship skills a sailor needs, one of the most important applies not to keeping the boat moving as fast as possible and in the right direction but to keeping it stationary. Cruising sailboats on wide-ranging voyages typically spend more time at anchor than they do sailing, and their crews need to know a variety of techniques for anchoring a boat securely in strong winds, adverse currents, deep water, shallow water, and in seabeds composed of rock, mud, sand or any combination thereof.

ANCHORS

For the level of sailing presented in *Sailing Made Easy*, you need to know the basics, just in case you need or want to anchor at some point. *Coastal Cruising Made Easy* covers anchoring techniques much more thoroughly.

Anchors come in many shapes, sizes, and weights to suit a variety of needs. Every boat should carry at least one, along with sufficient *rode*, the rope and/or chain that connects it to the boat, for it to be used in any anticipated depth of water. The boat on which you are learning to sail will normally be suitably equipped for the waters in which you are sailing. Make sure you know where the anchor is stowed, how to get it in the water safely, how much rode you need to pay out, and how to make the rode fast on deck.

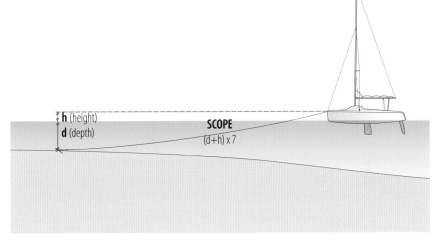

Calculate scope using the height of the bow above the water plus the depth of water where the anchor lies.

BASIC ANCHORING

Most anchors work by digging themselves into the seabed. To do this, they need the rode to pull at an angle closer to horizontal than to vertical. Obviously, then, you have to pay out more rode than it takes to simply get the anchor on the bottom.

Scope is the ratio of the length of rode let out to the depth of water. Normally, 7:1 scope is sufficient for a rope anchor rode. To arrive at the right length of rode to let out, you add the height of the boat's bow above the water to the depth. For example, if the depth is 10 feet and the freeboard at the bow is 4 feet, the length of rode needed for 7:1 scope will be $(10 + 4) \times 7 = 98$ feet.

The test for scope is the same as for sail trim: When in doubt, let it out.

Normally, you would approach your chosen spot for anchoring in much the same way you would a mooring buoy, by bringing the boat to a stop head to wind. Do this under mainsail alone or under motor. When the boat has stopped, lower the anchor and pay out the rode as the boat blows downwind. When you've let

out enough scope, make the rode fast. When the anchor takes hold, the boat will swing to the anchor and lie head to wind. If there's no wind, it will lie to the current.

On a small keelboat with no engine, one reason you might need to anchor is because the wind has died to nothing and you are drifting with the tide. By anchoring, you can stay in one place until the wind picks up or a launch from the sailing center comes to tow you home.

In such a situation, drop or furl the sails, lower the anchor, and pay out the required scope of rode. With no wind blowing the boat, the anchor should hold easily. Just avoid anchoring in a marked navigation channel.

To get under way when the wind comes back, raise the mainsail, let it luff while you haul back on the rode and lift the anchor, then sail off as you would from a mooring.

TIP *Stand well clear of the anchor rode when letting go the anchor — anchors are heavy, fall quickly through the water, and the rode can cause, at the least, a nasty rope burn.*

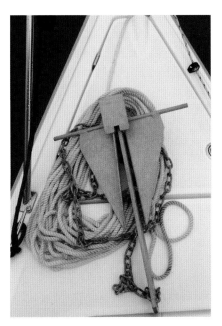

Typical ground tackle for a daysailing keelboat consists of a small anchor attached to a rope-and-chain rode.

MAN OVERBOARD

The call you never want to hear aboard any vessel at any time is, "Man overboard!" The idea of someone going for an accidental swim may seem funny, but every man overboard situation should be treated as a very serious matter, even in seemingly balmy conditions. In cold waters or cold weather, in restricted visibility or at nighttime, or in rough seas, the chances for a positive outcome diminish. Any delay in recovering the person in the water stacks the odds against his chances of survival. The best advice is to do all you can to prevent anyone from ever going overboard, but be prepared to handle the situation if it does occur.

FOCUS ON RECOVERY

If somebody does go overboard, the entire crew must focus on one goal: getting him back in the boat. To do that, you have to do four things as fast as possible but without causing further risk to the boat and the rest of the crew.
■ Keep the person overboard in sight.
■ Throw him a life ring or some other type of buoyant device.
■ Get the crew prepared for the recovery, return on a close reach, and stop the boat to windward of him and close enough to retrieve him.

■ Bring him back on board.
Sailors have developed several techniques for returning to a man overboard (MOB) and in any situation the exact one chosen will depend on the experience and skill of the crew, the number of crew on board, the type of boat, weather conditions, and perhaps other factors. In the end, all recovery techniques are more similar than different, as they all share the four key components mentioned above.

In this chapter, we'll look at two techniques for sailing a boat back to a

person in the water and stopping in a position from which to recover him. Both of them employ skills new sailors will have already been practicing.

Whatever return and recovery method you and your crew elect to use, your intial actions will be the same.

FIRST RESPONSE

The instant someone goes overboard, everyone and anyone who sees it happen should yell, "Man overboard!" ("Crew overboard!" works just fine too). The helmsman should designate a spotter to watch and never take his eyes off the MOB while the nearest crew throws the swimmer a flotation device. Anything that floats, such as a fender or a seat cushion, will work in a pinch, but ideally, your boat will have a Type IV throwable PFD easily accessible in the cockpit for first and fastest deployment. In rough weather and big waves, a MOB can disappear from sight within seconds. A field of floating objects near the MOB gives the spotter a better chance of keeping him in view, and any additional buoyancy will help him, especially if he is wearing a lot of clothes.

At the same time, one crewmember should find a long, sturdy line and tie into one end of it a bowline big enough to go around the torso of the MOB.

Throughout the maneuver that follows, the spotter never takes his eyes off the MOB, points toward him at all times, and communicates regularly with the helmsman, describing the MOB's location relative to the boat using both distance (e.g., "Three boat lengths") and direction (e.g., "Dead astern").

Even in relatively calm waters, a person in the water is not easy to spot in the first place, and the boat's maneuvers , in which it turns through 180 degrees and often more, make it difficult for the spotter to keep him in view.

THE FIGURE-EIGHT METHOD

You begin this maneuver by sailing away from the MOB. This may feel wrong, but the crew needs time to prepare the boat and recovery equipment and distance to be able to approach at the right point of sail, slowly, in control, and equipped to retrieve the MOB. While one crew prepares the line with the bowline, another can put in place some means of recovering the MOB, such as a boarding ladder.

① Bring the boat onto a beam reach and continue sailing away from the MOB. A distance of four to six boat lengths (20 to 30 seconds) should be sufficient — the distance will be shorter in lighter winds and longer in higher winds. While the boat is on a beam reach, the helmsman, guided by the spotter, glances back at the MOB two or three times while preparing the crew for the next maneuver.

② Tack the boat and sail back on a broad reach aiming a few boat lengths downwind of the MOB. Ease the jibsheet to reduce power.

③ Sail to a point from where you can head up onto a close reach aiming just slightly to windward of the MOB. Knowing exactly when to turn onto your final approach will take practice. You need enough distance on the close-reaching approach to slow the boat significantly before reaching the MOB.

....

TIP *Placing the boat just to windward of the MOB is considered the safest approach in most conditions. It will offer him some shelter from the wind and waves and make it easier to throw him a line. If you have overshot, luff the sails and the boat will blow downwind toward the MOB. Be especially careful, though, that you don't allow the boat to be blown on top of the MOB.*

....

④ Just as you did in your slowing drills near a buoy, sailing on a close reach, luff the mainsail to slow the boat to a crawl, but re-trim it to pick up speed if you are falling short of the MOB.

⑤ Come alongside the MOB at a speed of less than one knot, a very slow walking pace. Keep in mind that your ability to maneuver is limited, and once the boat stops altogether, you lose complete steering control.

⑥ As soon as you have gotten close to the MOB, your highest priority is to connect him to the boat with a line. Get the line with the bowline around his torso. DO NOT allow the boat to move away from the person in the water — the time expended making a second maneuver and approach could be costly.

⑦ Once connected to the MOB, turn the boat farther upwind to slow the boat and avoid blowing over the MOB. At this stage the boat will be hard to control. Expect a certain amount of chaos on board and stay focused on the priority of bringing the MOB into the boat.

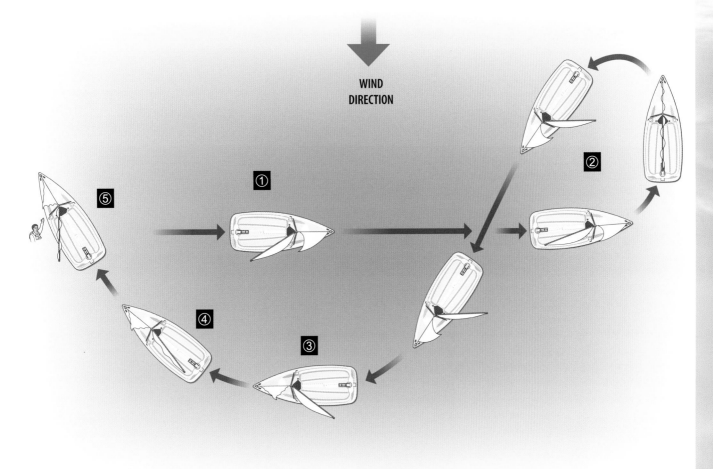

WIND
DIRECTION

THE BROAD REACH-CLOSE REACH METHOD

The Broad Reach-Close Reach Method of returning to an overboard victim simplifies the traditional Figure-Eight Method while emphasizing its strengths. Nicknamed the BRCR or "Bricker," it reduces the number of maneuvers involved. As with the Figure Eight or any MOB recovery method, perform all the same initial actions described earlier, such as throwing a life ring and designating a spotter.

① Fall off to a broad reach. Sail away only three to four boat lengths (15 to 20 seconds) to get maneuvering room.
② Head up and tack. Meanwhile, the crew prepares the boat and retrieval gear as before.
③ Working with the spotter, adjust your course to a close reach for the controlled slowing and approach just to windward of the MOB.
④ Repeat items 4 through 7 of the Figure-Eight Method.

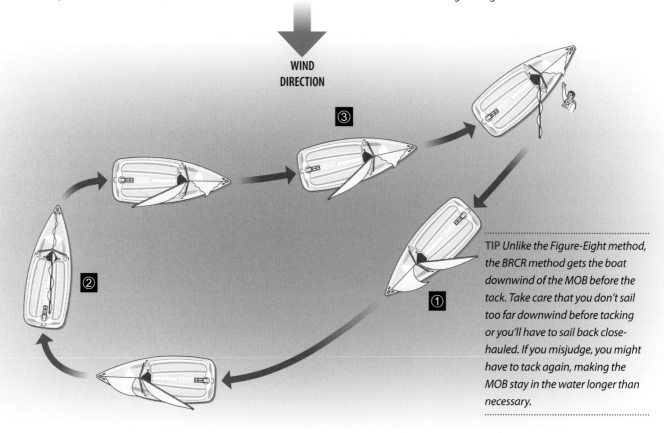

WIND
DIRECTION

③

②

①

TIP *Unlike the Figure-Eight method, the BRCR method gets the boat downwind of the MOB before the tack. Take care that you don't sail too far downwind before tacking or you'll have to sail back close-hauled. If you misjudge, you might have to tack again, making the MOB stay in the water longer than necessary.*

REPORTING INCIDENTS

Accidents happen, even to the most careful and competent sailors. If you are involved in an accident that results in injury or death or significant damage to property, you have a legal obligation to notify the proper authorities.

In the U.S., you are required to report to the state in which the accident occurred. You can do this through the city or county police, the sheriff, or a water-oriented agency such as the harbor patrol. In most cases, the United States Coast Guard (USCG) will not process boating accident reports but instead will direct a boater to the proper local authority. The USCG may provide onsite assistance, and may often be the first responder, especially when an incident threatens or results in death or serious injury, loss of a vessel, or a hazard to navigation.

The definition of significant damage or qualifying injury may vary between jurisdictions. As a conscientious sailor, you should know the laws that apply in your location and carry on board the contact information for the relevant authorities. Each state publishes its boating-safety regulations in pamphlet form and these are available in most outdoor-sports stores.

Prompt reporting and full cooperation with the authorities go a long way toward making the best of a difficult situation.

Select "textbook links" under the "sailing resources" section of www.asa.com for more information on reporting marine incidents.

RECOVERING A MAN OVERBOARD

Quick reactions, a sharp lookout, good teamwork among the crew, and diligent practice of the methods for sailing back to a MOB will ensure a quick return to his location. When you come alongside, you should be barely moving forward.

Once the crew has connected the MOB to the boat, the skipper, or the most experienced person remaining on board, has to decide how to retrieve him and coordinate the crew's actions. The most important factor in how you proceed is the condition of the MOB — whether he can help himself get back aboard the boat. A number of secondary factors, including the type of the boat, its size, and the strength of your crew, will also affect your choice of recovery method.

HELP THE VICTIM CLIMB ABOARD

If the MOB is conscious and able to assist in the process, the onboard crew might maneuver him to the swim step or ladder. Getting the MOB back aboard in this way will depend on sea conditions and his ability to climb.

PURE MUSCLE

If the combined strength of the crew is sufficient and the MOB light enough, the

Regular practice of the man-overboard drills in controlled conditions can be fun, while you hone skills and learn which techniques work best in which circumstances.

quickest way to retrieve the MOB might be for the onboard crew to simply grab hold of him by any means available — the rescue line, clothing, hands and arms — and physically heave him out of the water and onto the deck. This method best lends itself to small sailboats with low freeboard and plenty of crew.

USE A WINCH

Retrieving a larger MOB who cannot help himself may need more power than the crew alone can provide. A cockpit winch or a mast winch may provide sufficient mechanical advantage to hoist the MOB aboard. Use a cockpit winch on the opposite side of the boat to the MOB so that the bowline in the rescue line doesn't snarl the winch at the critical moment.

Whenever you use a winch, you must watch how you lead the line to it so as not to cause an override.

....

SAFETY TIP *Take care not to cause any further harm. You need to make sure the force exerted on the MOB doesn't pull him against the hull but pulls him safely upward.*

....

If you have a spare halyard, you could use it to raise the victim high enough to clear the lifelines. It might take some time and expertise to set up, but the more vertical hoisting angle would be better.

PRACTICE, PRACTICE, PRACTICE

Despite the variety of techniques for the middle stage as the boat turns back for the pick up, any MOB drill aboard a sailboat begins and ends with exactly the same steps. The methods share more similarities than differences.

You will learn more options as you progress with your sailing instruction, and they are discussed in *Coastal Cruising Made Easy*. But reading instructions for dealing with an emergency will only get you so far. Practice, with the entire crew, is crucial. Remember, the sooner you get back to your MOB, at a very slow speed and with the crew prepared for the retrieval, the better.

HYPOTHERMIA

On the face of it, hypothermia would appear to be an unlikely hazard when sailing on a warm sunny day, but it is a present danger with any marine activity, and especially when sailing in cold waters. Hypothermia is insidious, because if you don't recognize the early symptoms and take appropriate action, you won't realize your condition — your brain actually becomes numb — and without assistance, your condition can become life-threatening.

Prolonged exposure to wind, spray, and cold when on deck, and any length of time spent in the water, can elevate your chances of becoming hypothermic. Be alert to early indications in yourself and in your crewmates. The first sign of hypothermia is shivering. If left untreated and the person gets colder, further symptoms include clumsiness, apathy, confusion, and slurred speech. The victim may act as though in a stupor. The best defense against hypothermia is simply staying warm. On a sailboat that means keeping the layers of clothing

next to the body dry. If you ever have to recover a MOB, take precautionary measures against hypothermia.

Treating Hypothermia

If someone shows symptoms of hypothermia when you are out sailing:

■ Get the victim out of the cold wind (into the cabin if the boat has one). Have someone stay with him.

■ Remove the wet clothes, dry him off, and help him change into dry clothes and/or wrap a blanket (or a sailbag in a pinch) around his torso and head. Leave his limbs out of the wrap until his core has re-heated. Dry

his extremities and cover them lightly to reduce continued heat loss. The body's core will reheat the limbs naturally. Do not try to speed up the process.

■ Huddle around the victim to share body heat.

■ Head for shore where you'll have better resources to continue treatment.

■ A conscious victim who is able to swallow can start with small sips of tepid water, move to warm herbal tea or broth, and finally to hotter versions of the same liquids. Never administer alcohol to someone suffering from hypothermia.

PLANNING A DAY SAIL

Up until now, your time on the water has been occupied with learning the ropes and practicing techniques. Now it's time to apply your newly acquired skills and build on them while seeking new adventures under sail. Careful planning, even for a short sail, will ensure the trip passes safely and enjoyably.

WHERE

After successfully completing your first ASA sailing course, you will have learned to sail a familiar boat in familiar waters in light to moderate winds. Start small. Stay close to home and refine your skills in increments. As you spend more time on the water, you will gain experience, and as your knowledge of your local waters grows, so will your confidence to explore new areas.

Ask more-experienced sailors for advice. Study guidebooks of the area for ideas and set a goal. Begin in protected waters, maybe by picking an anchorage or restaurant to sail to for lunch and come back. Sailing to a destination, or around an island, will reward you with a measurable accomplishment.

HOW

Look at a *chart*, the nautical equivalent of a map, which you can obtain at any marine store. Even without any formal training, you can get a lot of information just from studying a chart. Examine the depths marked and you will understand the system behind aids to navigation and see areas to avoid because of the danger of grounding. Locate your departure point and your destination and determine a route between them that avoids hazards. Charts are among your most valuable planning tools.

WHEN

Weather and, if you are in a tidal area, tides, are key factors in your planning. Extreme winds or a strong current can make a close destination a long day's sail away. If tides and currents are a factor in your area, make sure you become familiar with them and how they can affect your sailing plans. Until you build more experience, avoid sailing in winds over 15 knots, or when whitecaps are prevalent.

As the weather and winds can be different on the water from on shore, it's wise to do a bit of homework. The web is a great place to get current information for your specific area. Select "textbook links" under the "sailing resources" section of www.asa.com to find current, local marine weather information. Ask local sailors which weather resources they use. In the United States, marine weather forecasts and warnings are transmitted on special VHF weather (Wx) channels. A VHF radio is invaluable on board. In some areas, storm advisory flags are displayed when the forecasted conditions are unsafe for small craft (and that often means big ones, too). Until you have a lot more experience, the red triangular small-craft-warning flag should be your sign to head back to shore.

If you are planning a sail, begin well ahead of time. Check the extended weather forecast and study the tide tables to pick a good sailing date. Continue to check the weather every day, to see if it's changing, and especially on the night before and the morning of your planned sail. Your crew will certainly appreciate it if you give them a last minute call to pack another layer of clothing!

Current, weather, and the time of dusk all determine how far you should sail before turning back for home port. Allow ample extra time for your sail back home — it's always easier to put the boat away in daylight.

Planning a sailing outing can be an adventure in itself. Charts provide an enormous amount of information.

FLOAT PLAN

Very simply, if you've told someone ashore your destination and when you expect to return, you've filed a float plan. The purpose of a float plan is to provide information that will be helpful to authorities and others in the event you get into difficulties. The more detailed and specific the information it contains, the more useful it will be.

Designate someone to be your shoreside contact. Provide him with your planned itinerary, a description of the boat, the number of people on board and their names, and your cell-phone information. Set a time at which this contact should begin to make calls, and specify to whom (the marina at your destination, for example) if you haven't checked in.

For your part, be sure to contact your shore person as soon as you have completed your journey or if you make any change in plan. If you have rented the boat, let the rental company know how to contact your person on shore.

Do not attempt to file a float plan with the USCG; it does not accept them.

WHO

The better the crew on board, the better your boat will sail. Try to find a crew with some sailing experience. Taking sailing school classmates as crew might be a good way to start. Friends and others with no knowledge of sailing will be fun passengers — and keen learners — but for safety and your own peace of mind, ensure you have some experienced crew on board as well. Involve your crew with the planning, so that they are aware of the options allowed by weather and tide.

WHAT

If you are renting a boat, it should have the required safety equipment aboard, but confirm that ahead of time. Expect it to have only the bare-essential gear for sailing and plan on bringing whatever else you need, including the charts you used for planning and some basic supplies for the crew.

Make sure you have enough food and water aboard, and consider bringing some extra jackets, warm clothing, and hats in case someone forgets theirs or the weather changes.

Advise your crew ahead of time as to what clothing and gear they should bring.

Other important but not legally required equipment to bring (or ensure is on board) for a daysail on a small keelboat includes:

- Tools
- Sponge
- Bailing device or pump
- Anchor and anchor rode
- Bucket
- Compass
- Knife
- First-aid kit
- Flashlight
- VHF radio
- Cell phone
- Air horn
- Whistle
- Lengths of strong lightweight line

STAYING COMFORTABLE AFLOAT — YOUR SAILING WARDROBE

The general rule for staying comfortable on a boat is to bring at least one more layer of clothes than you need on shore and to stay dry. Ultimately, your apparel will depend on three factors: the weather, the water temperature, and the size and type of boat.

Even if it's warm and sunny ashore, a brisk breeze blowing across cooler water accelerates heat loss. On a windy day, especially on a small, fast boat like a catamaran or dinghy, you'll get very wet just from the spray. And there's the risk of capsizing and a short swim. On a bigger keelboat, you are higher off the water and less spray will get on deck, so your clothing needs are often different.

When choosing your sailing apparel, keep in mind that the temperature afloat varies much more than it does on shore. One minute, you're sailing downwind, basking in the sun and the next you could be sailing upwind, with a cold breeze throwing spray on you. When sailing, dress in layers so you can easily stay comfortable through these changes of "season" on board.

The best way to stay warm on the water is to stay dry. That's why one of the most practical pieces of sailing gear is a water-resistant windbreaker jacket that is comfortable over a T-shirt or over a few inside layers.

If the conditions are wetter, a good set of foul weather gear is invaluable. Check out your local marine store to see all the options. Often, the basic chest-high overalls and jacket with a hood are the most versatile style. Bright colors will help the crew find you if you do happen to go for a swim.

HAVE FUN!

New sailors often expect a day sail to be as predictable as a Sunday drive, but sailing isn't about schedules. Keep your plans realistic. Don't try to go too far in a single day's sail and be prepared to modify your plan if the weather changes. Sailing, at its heart, isn't about destinations anyway, it's about being out on the water, learning new skills, and enjoying the challenge of facing the elements and wringing fun out of the wind. Remember that when you make your plan and you will enjoy your sailing adventures.

WELCOME, SAILOR

Maybe you noticed when you were out on the water that people on other boats waved at you as you sailed by. That's because sailors recognize their fellows as being part of a special group. While the connection is evidently social, it's also built upon a shared dependency.

The sea can be as challenging as it is alluring, and seafarers have since time immemorial shared a mutual respect for it and looked out for each others' welfare. In fact, this tradition, of rendering assistance at sea to fellow sailors in need, is now written into maritime law.

Now you are a sailor, you have joined this special community. Whether sailing develops into part of your lifestyle or becomes your lifestyle, you have opened the door to a world of new adventures. You will never lack the company of likeminded people, with common aspirations and interests, anywhere in the world you sail.

While you've learned a great deal in *Sailing Made Easy*, your journey is just beginning. We'll teach you the new skills you'll need as you begin to sail farther from home in *Coastal Cruising Made Easy*. See you on the water!

PERSONAL GEAR

Tips about what personal gear to bring, or not to bring, on a sailboat.
- Sunglasses, hat, and sunscreen — every time you sail. The sails and water intensify the glare of the sun.
- Comfortable sailing shoes with white rubber non-slip soles.
- Sailing gloves — some people find handling the lines more comfortable with these. Make sure they are a good fit.
- Extra dry clothes, including shoes and socks, stored in a waterproof bag. (If there's no room for them on the boat, you'll be glad to have dry clothes ready in your car at the end of your sail).
- A folding knife — you never know when you might need to cut a rope.
- Life jacket — if you find one that you like to wear, bring it every time you go sailing, even if the boat has its own gear. It only "works" when you are wearing it.
- Cell phone — it's a good idea to have at least one aboard in case you want to call the marina. You could also use it to call for assistance, but only if your sailboat is not equipped with a VHF radio. Store the cell phone in a waterproof bag, preferably one that floats.
- Rings — if you wear finger rings, consider leaving them ashore as they can be dangerous if they catch a line.

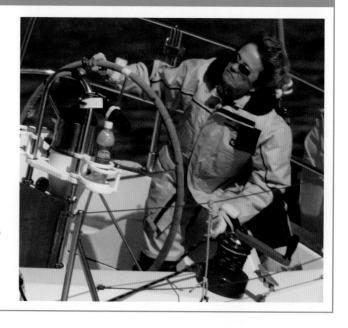

REVIEW QUESTIONS (see page 126 for answers)

FILL IN THE BLANK OR MATCH THE LETTER WITH THE WORD

1 In the Navigation Rules, Rule 5 (the "Lookout Rule") requires all vessels to maintain a proper lookout using _____ and _____ and any other available means (e.g., radar).

2 It is the responsibility of every vessel operator to avoid a _____ .

3 The _____ - _____ vessel's obligation is to maintain _____ and speed.

4 The _____ - _____ vessel is required to maneuver out of the way of the stand-on vessel.

5 A vessel overtaking another vessel must _____ _____ to the vessel being overtaken (see diagram).

6 When two sailing vessels are approaching on opposite tacks, the vessel with the wind on the _____ side is the stand-on vessel (see diagram).

7 When two vessels are sailing with the wind on the same side, the vessel to _____ is the give-way vessel (see diagram).

8 When a sailboat has its engine running and in gear, it is defined as a _____ - _____ vessel, regardless of whether the sails are raised.

9 A powerboat, not in a channel or restricted in its ability to maneuver, should _____ _____ to a sailboat under sail, unless the sailboat is _____ the powerboat.

10 When two power-driven vessels are meeting head-on, _____ boat is the stand-on vessel. Instead, both vessels should alter course to _____ and pass port-to-port (see diagram).

11 In a crossing situation, if powerboat A sees powerboat B on its starboard side, then powerboat A shall _____ _____ (see diagram).

12 The give-way vessel shall take _____ and _____ action to keep clear. If the give-way vessel does not seem to be taking early or substantial enough action, then the _____ - _____ vessel must take action to avoid the collision.

13 Nearly all vessels must be _____ with the state in which they operate, and/or _____ through the U.S. Coast Guard Vessel Documentation Center.

14 There must be at least one Type I, II, III, or V _____ _____ on board for _____ person.

15 Examples of visual distress signals include:

a _____

b _____ _____

c _____ _____

d _____ _____ _____

16 An _____ _____ can serve as a sound-producing device.

17 Any sailboat under 26 feet in length with an engine must carry a _____ _____ .

18 A sailing vessel over 23 feet in length under way at night or in restricted visibilty is required to display a _____ sidelight on the port side, a green sidelight on the _____ side, and a _____ light on the stern.

19 When a sailboat 23 feet or longer is navigating at night with its engine operating in gear it must also display a white _____ light in addition to the sidelights and stern light.

20 The Federal limit for blood alcohol content is _____ percent.

21 In the Aids to Navigation system, a _____ is a floating aid anchored to the bottom. A beacon is a _____ mark and can be on land or in the water.

22 Lateral Aids to Navigation are identified by three features, _____ , _____ , and _____ .

23 A way to remember on which side to keep the starboard-hand (red) markers when entering a channel from seaward is the phrase " _____ _____ _____ ."

24 A _____ _____ buoy has red and white vertical stripes and is safe to pass on either side.

25 The procedure for recovering a crewmember who has fallen overboard (a MOB), is:

 a Appoint someone as a _____ to keep the MOB in sight.

 b Throw _____ device(s) to the MOB.

 c Maneuver the boat back to the MOB and approach on a _____ _____ point of sail.

 d Stop the boat by _____ the sails and bring the MOB aboard.

26 The Figure-8 recovery method works well on small boats since there is no _____ , thereby reducing the risk of a second MOB.

27 Checking the _____ forecast is one of the most important steps to take before going sailing.

28 A _____ plan can be provided to a friend or relative who is willing to be responsible for contacting the authorities if you do not make contact on schedule.

5 Vessels overtaking

6 Sailboats on opposite tacks

7 Sailboats on same tack

10 Powerboats meeting

11 Powerboats crossing

APPENDIX

THE OUTBOARD MOTOR

Many sailboats used for teaching the ASA Basic Keelboat Standard are equipped with outboard motors, which students must learn to use for certain situations. While the proper operation of an outboard engine is not a part of this Standard, for the benefit of these students, we chose to "borrow" the outboard section from the next book in our series, *Coastal Cruising Made Easy*, and include it as an appendix.

Outboard motors are attached to sailboats in a variety of ways. This one is on a lifting bracket on the transom.

OUTBOARD BASICS

Sailboats and outboard motors can be a bit of an awkward mix. Unless the boat has been specifically designed around efficient and easy use of an outboard, operating it is sometimes a little tricky. Still, the great value of outboards is that they help many sailors use their boats to the fullest.

Outboards on sailboats don't get much above 15 horsepower. This is also about the maximum size of motor found on dinghies used in conjunction with cruising sailboats, so it's well worth taking a look at how they work and how to operate them.

MOTOR ATTACHMENT

Almost all outboards have a clamp frame that attaches to the boat with screw clamps. In the case of a dinghy, the motor clamps directly to the transom. Sailboats can have a variety of arrangements, from a built-in outboard well in the cockpit to an adjustable bracket bolted to the transom to which the motor is then clamped. The clamping mechanism allows the motor to be easily detached from the boat for storage and maintenance (and to deter theft).

A mechanism on the clamp frame allows the motor to be tilted. When in use, the motor is latched in an upright position with the propeller in the water. When it's not being used for propulsion, the motor can be tilted and latched with the propeller out of the water.

MOTOR CONTROLS

Anyone familiar with gasoline-powered yard tools will recognize most of the standard features of an outboard motor.

Older outboards have two-stroke engines that require oil to be mixed with the gasoline. Newer models have four-stroke engines that don't require oil in the fuel but are markedly heavier.

Starting is effected by pulling a cord. The fuel line has a squeeze bulb for priming the carburetor before starting, and a choke (either manual or automatic) controls the air and fuel mixture for starting. A kill button stops the motor by cutting off the ignition spark.

In addition to these controls, the outboard has a tiller (used to steer the boat by rotating the motor within the clamp frame), a throttle (usually a twist type like that on a motorcycle) on the end of the tiller, and a gearshift lever, which might be on the side of the motor or at the root of the tiller.

GASOLINE FUEL

Outboard motors burn gasoline, which has to be handled carefully because of its flammable nature. Many small motors have a built-in fuel tank. More powerful (and more thirsty) motors are used in conjunction with a separate larger, and usually portable fuel tank. To prevent gasoline or its fumes from getting belowdecks, this fuel tank should be stowed on deck or in a cockpit locker that's sealed from the boat's interior and drains overboard.

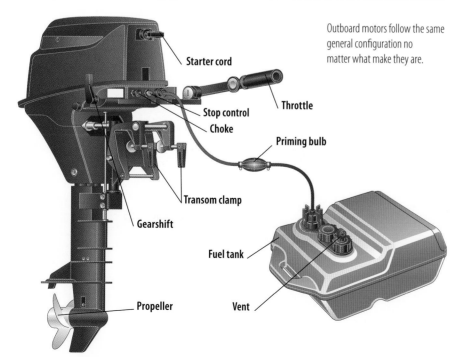

Outboard motors follow the same general configuration no matter what make they are.

Starter cord

Throttle

Stop control

Choke

Priming bulb

Transom clamp

Gearshift

Fuel tank

Propeller

Vent

STARTING AN OUTBOARD MOTOR

While you will encounter some differences between outboard motors, mostly related to size or antiquity, they all operate in generally the same way, so the starting sequence is fairly universal.

PRE-START SEQUENCE

① Check that the motor clamps are drawn up tightly against the transom or bracket — a loose motor might fall off.

② If the motor has been tilted out of the water, disengage the tilt lock, lower the motor all the way down, and lock it.

③ Check the fuel supply. If the motor has an integral tank, unscrew the fill cap and peer in. A separate tank will have a gauge on the top. On a four-stroke motor, check the engine-oil level.

④ Open the vent on top of the fill cap (on the motor or on the tank) by unscrewing it counterclockwise.

....

TIP *If you forget to open the vent, a partial vacuum will form in the tank, preventing the motor from drawing fuel, and the motor will stop, probably at an awkward moment.*

....

⑤ Connect the fuel hose from an external tank to the motor or, on a motor with an integral tank, open the fuel valve.

⑥ Locate the priming bulb. With an external tank it's in the fuel line. Pump fuel to the carburetor by squeezing the bulb four or five times or until it feels firm. Don't overdo it or you risk flooding and the motor won't start.

⑦ Work the gearshift and ensure it's in neutral.

⑧ Set the throttle to the "start" position.

⑨ If the motor has a manual choke, set it in the "start" position.

⑩ If the motor has a safety tab, make sure it's attached to the kill button, otherwise, the motor will not start. Before you start the engine, double check that it's locked down and that no line can get into the prop.

....

TIP *The safety tab is on a tether. If the outboard is on a dinghy, clip the tether to your clothing or around your wrist so if you fall out of the boat, you'll pull out the tab, the engine will stop, and you'll be able to recover the dinghy (and yourself).*

....

STARTING SEQUENCE

① Brace yourself in a position from which you can pull squarely on the starter cord.

This outboard has the gearshift on the front.

② Gently pull the starter cord until you feel the gears in the mechanism engage. A hard yank could damage the gears.

③ Pull out firmly on the starter cord until it's extended two to three feet (not until it stops, as that might cause it to break). Don't let go, but ease the cord toward the motor as it rewinds itself back into its spool.

④ If the motor doesn't start on the first pull, repeat steps 2 and 3. You may need to adjust the choke and/or throttle to get the motor to fire.

⑤ When the motor starts, let it run at starting speed for a few seconds, then throttle back to idle.

⑥ Look for a stream of cooling water exiting the back of the motor. If you don't see one, stop the motor by pushing the stop button. Without cooling water, the engine will overheat.

⑦ When the motor has warmed up enough, usually within 20 seconds, push in the choke (if the motor has one).

⑧ With the boat still secured to the dock (or to the mother ship if you're in the dinghy), and the motor idling, shift briefly into forward and reverse gears to ensure they are working properly.

....

SAFETY TIP *Look behind you before you pull the starter cord and don't heave on it wildly — your elbow could end up in a crewmate's eye or you could lose your balance and fall out of the boat.*

....

Whether on a dinghy or a sailboat, start an outboard motor from a position where you are secure and nothing will obstruct your movements. Note the fuel-tank cap on the top of this motor . . . and the very long starter cord!

MANEUVERING A SAILBOAT WITH AN OUTBOARD

Many sailboats up to about 25 feet are powered by outboard motors. On some boats, the motor is fixed, and the boat is always steered with its rudder. On others, the motor is mounted so it can be used to steer the boat, which has some advantages when maneuvering around docks. With the motor in gear, the rotating propeller generates thrust by pushing water away. This "jet" of water is called prop wash, and you can change its direction by turning the motor with its tiller.

Once under way and in open water, it's often more practical to steer the boat with the rudder than with the outboard.

BOAT SPEED AND STEERING

A rudder cannot turn a boat that is not moving through the water. An outboard motor that can be turned can be used to rotate a boat that has no forward (or sternward) motion.

When you rotate an outboard, you change the direction of its prop wash.

With the outboard in forward gear, the result is similar to turning the rudder to deflect the prop wash from an inboard engine. When you push the outboard's tiller to port, the boat's bow turns to starboard (and vice versa).

In reverse gear, the result is dramatically different. By turning the motor, you can direct the prop wash so as to push the stern of the boat in the direction you want it to go. When you push the outboard's tiller to port, the prop wash pushes the boat's stern to starboard.

Once the boat gains speed (how much speed will vary from boat to boat) the rudder becomes the better means with which to steer it.

On some sailboats, you can't reach the outboard from the helm. This means that when maneuvering in close quarters, such as when leaving or entering a dock, you have to steer with the outboard while you operate the throttle and gearshift. While doing so, you'll want the boat's helm secured amidships.

When you reach open water and expect to motor at a steady speed for a while, set the throttle where you want it, align the outboard fore-and-aft, and steer with the boat's rudder.

To gain confidence using the outboard, take the sailboat to an area where you can maneuver freely without interfering with other boats and try some exercises.

RUDDER STEERING

① Get the boat moving in a straight line at a comfortable speed and set the outboard fore and aft.
② Using the boat's helm, steer the boat slowly to starboard, then to port.
③ Use more helm to turn the boat harder, first to starboard, then to port.

④ After getting a feel for how the boat responds, turn it in a circle.

⑤ Resume your original course.

OUTBOARD STEERING

① Start with the boat moving on a steady course.

② Have someone hold the helm so the rudder is fore-and-aft.

③ Turn the outboard a little at a time to steer the boat to starboard, then to port.

④ Turn the outboard more to turn the boat more sharply.

⑤ After getting a feel for how the boat responds, turn it in a circle.

⑥ Resume your original course

TRIAL MANEUVERS

You could further experiment by doing the exercises at different speeds, which would give you valuable insights into how the boat will handle in a range of situations. To operate the throttle and gearshift, though, you need to be within reach of the outboard motor. Whenever you are in a situation where you might need to slow down, stop, or take quick action, drive and steer with the outboard.

STOPPING WITH AN OUTBOARD

Outboard motor propellers typically have less "bite" in reverse than in forward, so are not very effective at stopping the boat quickly. Unless the motor is fixed, you don't have to cope with prop walk, as you would with an inboard engine, because you can direct the prop wash to push the stern in the direction you want it to go.

When approaching a dock or a mooring, do so slowly. Using bursts of forward thrust to keep the boat moving is better than trying to stop the boat by using reverse.

OPERATING IN REVERSE

Whenever you want a sailboat to move backward you must have a firm hand on the helm to hold the rudder straight. Now, you effectively have two helms to control so, if steering with the outboard, have someone hold the boat's helm so the rudder is fore and aft.

Using an outboard, when starting from a full stop, you can turn the motor so the prop wash pushes the stern in the direction you want it to go.

As a rule, sailboats are not happy moving stern first. If you have to go astern (when entering or leaving a slip, for example), do so as slowly as you can while maintaining steering control and for as short a distance as possible.

UNDER SAIL

An outboard motor dragging behind the boat slows you down when sailing, and that's not fun! As soon as you have set the mainsail, shut down the motor, tilt it up, and lock it in that position.

When done sailing, and before you drop the mainsail, you might want to lower the motor and start it. You can then use it to hold the boat head to wind while you drop and furl the sail.

Note that the outboard motor is in the tilted-up position while this sailboat is under sail.

GLOSSARY

A

Aback Of a sail, when the wind is on the "wrong" side

Abaft Toward the *stern*, as in "abaft the *beam*"

Abeam Off the boat at right angles to its centerline

Aft Toward the *stern* or behind the boat

After Toward the *stern*

Aground When the *hull* or *keel* is touching the *bottom*

Aid to navigation A *buoy* or other device deployed to mark a *channel*, a *navigational* feature, or a hazard

Aloft Above the *deck*, usually in the *rig*

Amidships At or toward the middle of the boat

Anchor A device lowered to the *bottom* while *secured* to the boat to hold the boat stationary

Apparent wind The combination of *true wind* and the wind effect of motion as felt aboard a moving boat

Astern Behind the *stern*

Athwartships Across the boat from side to side

B

Backing The act of setting a sail *aback*

Backstay A wire support from the top of the *mast* to the *stern*

Backwinding similar to *backing*

Ballast Weight placed low in the boat to give it stability

Batten A slat inserted in the *leech* of a sail to support the *sailcloth*

Batten pocket A pocket sewn into the sail to hold a *batten*

Beacon An *aid to navigation* that's fixed in place

Beam (1) The width of a boat at its widest point

Beam (2) The region of the boat's sides halfway between *bow* and *stern*

Beam reach The *point of sail* where the wind is *abeam* of the boat

Bear away To turn the boat away from the wind, *fall off*

Beat, beating To sail to windward *close-hauled*

Bend A *knot* used to tie a *line* to another line or to an object

Bend on To attach, as a sail to a *spar*

Blanketed Hidden from the wind, as when one sail is blanketed by another

Block A pulley

Boathook A pole with a hook on one end useful for snagging a *line* or a ring

Bolt rope A rope sewn into the edge of a sail, often used to attach it to the *mast* or *boom*

Bottom The seabed or bed under any body of water

Boom The *spar* that supports the *foot* of the *mainsail*

Boom vang An item of *running rigging*, often a *block* and *tackle*, used to hold down the *boom*

Bow The *forward* part of a boat

Bowline A *knot* that forms a loop in the end of a *line*

Bow line A *dock line* tied between the *bow* of a boat and a *dock*

Broad reach The *point of sail* between a *beam reach* and a *run*

Buoy A floating object anchored to the *bottom*

By the lee Sailing on a *run* with the wind on the same side as the *mainsail*

C

Cabin The interior of a boat

Cam cleat A *fitting* with spring-loaded jaws used to *secure* a *line*

Can buoy A cylindrical *buoy* used as an *aid to navigation*

Capsize To turn over

Cast off To undo completely a *line* that has been *secured*

Catamaran A boat with two *hulls*

Centerboard A board that pivots down from the bottom of the boat to provide sideways resistance

Chafe Damage caused to a sail or a *line* by rubbing

Chafing gear Material used to prevent *chafe*

Chainplate Metal fabrication attached to the *hull* and to which a *stay* or *shroud* is connected

Channel A narrow passage; a deeper-water route often marked with *aids to navigation*

Chart A nautical map

Chock A fixed *fairlead* through which *dock lines* are led

Cleat A fitting used to *secure* a *line* under load

Clew The *aft* lower corner of a sail

Close-hauled The *point of sail* where a boat sails as close to the wind as possible

Close reach The *point of sail* between *close-hauled* and a *beam reach*

Cockpit The area of the boat, usually recessed into the *deck*, from which the boat is steered and sailed

Coil (1) To make up a *line* into tidy loops

Coil (2) A *line* that has been *coiled*

Come about to *tack*

Companionway The entrance from the *cockpit* or *deck* to the *cabin*

Course The direction in which a boat is being steered

Cringle An eye formed by sewing a rope or metal ring into, e.g., a sail

Cunningham A line used to tension the *luff* of a sail

D

Daggerboard A board that lowers vertically down from the bottom of the boat to provide sideways resistance

Deck The generally horizontal surface that encloses the top of the *hull*

Dinghy A small boat

Dock (1) A place where a vessel is berthed, but generally used to refer to the pier, quay, or pontoon to which it's tied when in that berth

Dock (2) To bring a boat to its *dock*

Dock line A *line* used to tie a boat in its *dock*

Docking The process of bringing a boat into its *dock*

Downhaul A *line* used to tension the *luff* of a sail by pulling down the *boom* at the *gooseneck*

Downwind In the direction toward which the wind is blowing

Draft (1) The depth of a boat below the water

Draft (2) The curvature of a sail

E

Ease To let out a *line* that has load on it

Eye of the wind Directly to *windward*

F

Fair Smooth, unobstructed

Fairlead A *fitting* used to lead a *line* fair and at the correct angle to a *winch*, *cleat*, or other *fitting*.

Fake, flake To lay out a *line* in parallel lengths so it can run freely

Fall off To turn away from the wind, *bear away*

Fender A cushion, usually an inflated cylinder of rubber or similar material, placed between a boat and a *dock*

Fitting A piece of hardware that is fixed to the boat or its *spars*

Flake To lay in even loose folds, as a sail

Foot The bottom edge of a sail

Fore-and-aft The direction parallel with the centerline of a boat

Foredeck The *forward* part of the *deck*, usually forward of the forwardmost *mast*

Foresail A sail set *forward* of the *mainsail*, often a *jib* or a *headsail*

Forestay A *stay* that supports the *mast* from *forward*

Forward Toward the *bow*

Fouled Tangled, snagged

Freeboard The height of the *hull* above the *waterline*

Full About a sail, when it is not flapping or *luffing*

Furl To stow a sail on a spar or a stay

G

Gear General term for equipment aboard a sailboat

Genoa A large *jib* that extends *aft* of the *mast*

Give-way vessel Under the *Navigation Rules*, the *vessel* that is obliged to adjust its *course* or speed to avoid collision with another vessel

Going astern To be moving backwards

Gooseneck An articulated fitting that connects a *boom* to a *mast*

Grommet A metal ring set into a sail

Ground tackle Collective term for a boat's *anchors* and their *rodes*

Gunwale The top edge of the *deck* where it joins the *hull*

Gust An increase in wind speed that lasts just a short while

H

Halyard A *line* used to raise and lower a sail

Hank A metal clip or fabric tab used to attach a sail's *luff* to a *stay*

"Hard a-lee!" The announcement by the *helmsman* that he is about to *tack* the boat

Hatch A covered opening in the *deck*

Head The top of a sail

Head to wind A boat's position when its *bow* is pointing directly into the wind

Headboard A reinforcement at the *head* of a sail

Head down To steer away from the wind, *bear away*, *fall off*

Headfoil A metal or plastic cover that fits over a *forestay* to accept the *luff tape* of a *jib* when it's *hoisted*

Headsail Any sail set *forward* of the forwardmost *mast*; a *jib*

Headstay The *stay* between the top of the *mast* and the *bow*

Head up To steer more toward the wind

Headway Motion forward

Heave-to To hold a boat almost stationary by setting the sails and *rudder* in opposition

Heel (Of a boat) to lean sidways under the pressure of the wind on the sails

Helm The *tiller* or wheel with which the boat is steered

Helmsman The person at the *helm* steering the boat

Hiking stick An extension to the *tiller* that allows the *helmsman* more freedom of movement

Hitch A type of *knot*, used to attach a *line* to an object or to another line

Hoist To haul *aloft*

Hull The watertight structural shell of a boat.

I

Inboard Toward the centerline of the boat; inside the *hull*

In irons Of a boat that's *head to wind*, having lost all *headway*

J

Jammer A device that holds a *line* by an internal mechanism

Jib A triangular sail set *forward* of the *mainmast*

Jibe To turn the boat so that its *stern* passes through the wind

"Jibe-ho!" Announcement by the *helmsman* that he is about to steer the boat into a *jibe*; also a warning that an accidental jibe is imminent

Jibsheet A *line* attached to the *clew* of a *jib* used to adjust its angle to the wind

Jump When hoisting a sail, to haul on the *halyard* at the *mast*

K

Keel The main structural member along the bottom of a boat's *hull*; on a sailboat often an appended fin-shaped structure that contains *ballast*

Keelboat A sailboat that has a *keel* and *ballast*, usually combined

Knot (1) A fastening made by entwining a rope, *line*, or cord with itself or with other ropes, lines, or cords

Knot (2) Unit of speed: one nautical mile (6,076 feet) per hour

L

Lay Of a rope's strands, the direction they are twisted, as in right-hand or left-hand

Lazy Of, for example, a *jibsheet*, the windward one that's not under load

Leech The *after* edge of a sail

Lee Sheltered area to *leeward* of something (boat, building, island) that's protected from the wind

Lee helm The tendency of a sailboat when sailing to turn away from the wind

Lee side The side away from the wind, or *downwind* side

Leeward The direction, or side of the boat, away from the wind

Lifeline A wire supported on *stanchions* around the perimeter of the *deck* to prevent crew from falling overboard

Line A length of *rope* that serves a specific purpose on board

Locker A storage compartment

Loose footed Of a *mainsail*, for example, that is attached to its *boom* at its *tack* and *clew* but not along its *foot*

Luff (1) The *forward* edge of a sail

Luff (2) The fluttering of a sail when the boat is too close to the wind for the sail's *trim*

Luff (3) To *head up* so that the sails *luff*

Luff tape Tape with an integral *bolt rope* that is sewn to the *luff* of a sail

M

Main boom The *boom* that supports the *mainsail*

Mainmast The principal *mast* on a sailboat

Mainsail The sail attached to the *aft* side of the *mainmast*

Mainsheet The line used to control the main *boom* and thus also to *trim* the *mainsail*

Make fast To *secure*, as when tying a *line* to a *cleat*

Mark General term for an *aid to navigation*

Mast A fixed vertical *spar* that holds up a sail or sails

Masthead fly A wind vane fitted at the masthead

Moor To tie up (a boat)

Mooring A permanently set *anchor*

Mooring buoy A *buoy* attached to a *mooring* and to which a boat can be *moored*

Multihull A boat with more than one *hull*

N

Navigate To conduct a *vessel*'s passage on a body of water

Navigation The act of *navigating*

Navigational chart A map used for the purpose of *navigation*

Navigation light A light required under the *Navigation Rules* when a *vessel* is operating at night or in poor visibility

Navigation Rules Laws established to prevent collisions on the water

No-sail zone The zone in relation to the wind where the sails cannot generate power

Nun buoy A *buoy* with a cone-shaped top used as an *aid to navigation*

O

Off the wind Any *point of sail* where the wind is *abaft* the *beam*

On the wind Any *point of sail* where the wind is *forward* of the *beam*

Outboard (1) Away from the centerline of a boat; outside the *gunwale*

Outboard (2) A portable motor that attaches (usually) to the *stern* of a boat

Outhaul A *line* used to tension the *foot* of the *mainsail*

P

Pier A structure built over the water on pilings

Pinch To sail too close to the wind, so that the sails *luff*

Pontoon A *moored* floating structure to which a boat can be tied

Point of sail The direction a boat is sailing relative to the wind

Port (1) A harbor

Port (2) The left-hand side of a boat when facing *forward*

Port tack Any course where the wind is blowing on the *port* side of the boat

Puff An increase of wind strength of short duration, usually with less strength than a *gust*

Pulpit A guardrail at the bow or stern of a boat to which (usually) the *lifelines* are connected

Q

Quarter The sides of a boat between the *beam* and the *stern*

Quay A solid structure to which vessels tie up to load and unload

R

Reach Any *point of sail* between *close-hauled* and a *run*

"Ready about!" The command used to signal the crew to prepare to *tack*

Reef (1) An area of rock or coral, usually submerged, that presents a hazard to *navigation*

Reef (2) To reduce the area of a sail that is exposed to the wind

Rig (1) To attach, as a sail

Rig (2) The total assembly of sails, *spars*, and *rigging* aboard a sailboat

Rigging Wires and *lines* used to support *spars* and to control sails

Rode The *line* and/or chain that connects an *anchor* to the boat

Roller furling A mechanism for *furling* a sail by rolling it around its *stay*

Rope To a sailor, raw material for making up *lines*

Round up Of a boat, to spontaneously turn *head to wind*

Rudder The movable appendage attached to a boat under the water and with which it can be steered

Run The *point of sail* on which the wind is *aft*

Running rigging The adjustable *rigging* used to raise and lower or *trim* the sails

S

Sail tie Length of webbing used to *secure* sails

Sailboard A sailboat that is essentially a surfboard with a sail

Sailcloth Material from which sails are made

Sailing by the lee Sailing on a *run* with the wind on the same side of the boat as the *mainsail*

Scope The ratio of the length of *anchor rode* deployed to the vertical distance from the boat's *bow* to the *bottom*

Secure (1) To *make fast* (as a *line*)

Secure (2) To make safe

Self-tailer A device on a *winch* that enables it to grasp and gather the *tail* of a *line* as it is wound in on the winch

Shackle A closable metal connector used in *rigging*

Shackle key A tool for tightening and loosening a *shackle*

Sheet A *line* used to control the alignment of a sail relative to the boat and the wind

Shroud A wire that provides *athwartships* support to the *mast*

Sidelight A *navigation light* that shines on one side of the boat in an arc from the *bow* to 22.5 degrees *abaft* the *beam*

Slip A berth where a boat *docks* between *piers*, *pontoons*, or pilings

Sloop A sailboat with one *mast*, a *mainsail*, and one *headsail*

Snub To hold a *line* under tension by wrapping it around a *cleat* or a *winch*

Spar A pole used to support a sail, e.g. *mast*, *boom*

Spinnaker A large, lightweight, rounded sail used when sailing *downwind*

Spreader An *athwartships* strut on a *mast* that holds a *shroud* away from the *mast*

Stanchion A metal post that supports *lifelines*

Standing rigging *Rigging*, e.g. *shrouds* and *stays*, that supports *spars* and that remains in place when a boat is not sailing

Stand-on vessel In a situation when two *vessels* converge, the vessel that must maintain its *course* and speed

Starboard The right-hand side of a boat when looking *forward*

Starboard tack Any *course* where the wind is blowing on the *starboard* side of the boat

Stay A piece of *standing rigging* that supports a *mast* in the *fore-and-aft* direction

Steaming light A *navigation light* that shines on both sides of the boat in an arc from the *bow* to 22.5 degrees *abaft* the *beam*; used on a sailing vessel that is under power

Stern The *aft* part of a boat

Stern light A *navigation light* that shines on both sides of the boat in an arc from the *stern* to 22.5 degrees *abaft* the *beam*

Stow To put away in a seamanlike manner

Stripping arm Part of a *self-tailer*

Surge To *ease* a loaded line while *snubbing* it to keep it under control

T

Tack (1) The *forward* lower corner of a sail

Tack (2) To change *course* by turning the *bow* of the boat through the wind

Tack (3) A *course* designation according to which side of the boat (*port* or *starboard*) the wind is blowing onto

Tackle A *line* reeved through a series of *blocks* to gain mechanical advantage

Tail (1) The end of a *working line* (e.g. *halyard*, *sheet*) after the *winch* or *snubber* that is taking the load

Tail (2) To pull on the *tail* of a *line*

Tail bag A bag in which *line tails* are *stowed* to keep them tidy

Telltale A short length of light yarn or similar material attached to a sail to indicate the flow of air across it and thus the state of the sail's *trim*

Tide The movement of a body of water caused by the gravitational effects of the moon and sun

Tiller A lever used to control the angle of the *rudder* and thereby steer the boat

Topping lift A *line* or wire that supports a *boom* when it is not being supported by its sail

Transom The more or less flat surface that closes the *hull* at the *stern*

Traveler A car-and-track system that allows the *mainsheet*'s attachment point to the *deck* to be moved *athwartships*

Trim (1) To adjust a sail by hauling in on the *sheet*

Trim (2) The position a sail is set relative to the wind

Trimaran A *vessel* with three *hulls*

True wind The wind as observed at a stationary point

U

Upwind In the direction from which the wind is blowing

V

Vang A piece of *running rigging* used to restrain a *spar*, e.g. *boom vang*

Vessel Used as an all-inclusive term in the *Navigation Rules* to describe any ship or boat or craft capable of being *navigated*

W

Waterline The line around the interface between the *hull* and the surface of the water

Weather side The side of a boat from which the wind is blowing; *windward* side

Weather helm The tendency of a boat when sailing to *head up* into the wind

Winch A device consisting of a gear-driven drum that is operated with a handle to provide mechanical advantage when hauling on a *line*; also used to *snub* a line

Windage The resistance a boat's *hull*, *rig*, and superstructure present to the wind

Windward Toward the wind

Windward side The side upon which the wind is blowing

Wing on wing Sailing on a *run* with the *jib* and *mainsail* set on opposite sides of the boat

Winging the jib Sailing *wing on wing*

Working Of a *sheet*, the one that is currently being used to *trim* the sail

Z

Zephyr A gentle breeze, perfect for a quiet evening sail

INDEX

Bold entries show illustrations or diagrams.

ANSWERS TO REVIEW QUESTIONS

SAILING — OPEN UP YOUR WORLD page 26 answers

1 speed, direction
2 lift
3 no-sail zone
4 zigzag
5 close-hauled
6 reaching
7 running
8 angle (or trim)
9 apparent
10 keel
11 rudder, tiller, steering wheel
12
  k hull
  c deck
  i cockpit
  a transom
  f bow
  h stern
  e rudder
  d helm (tiller or wheel)
  b stanchion
  g lifeline
  j pulpit
13 The Sailboat's Rig
  d mast
  a boom
  k gooseneck
  m spreader
  h shroud
  n headstay/forestay
  l backstay
  b mainsail
  i headsail/jib
  f halyard
  e mainsheet
  c jibsheet
  g boom vang
  j boom topping lift
14 Parts of a Sail
  g head
  a tack
  d clew
  c luff
  f leech
  e foot
  b batten

15 On-Board Orientation
  a port
  f starboard
  c forward
  g aft
  h ahead
  i abeam
  e astern
  b windward
  d leeward

GETTING A FEEL FOR SAILING page 56 answers

1 head, wind
2 trimmed
3 eased
4 luffing
5 shore, landmark
6 heading up
7 bearing away
8 doubt, out
9 in irons
10
  a close reach
  b broad reach
  c close-hauled
  d run
  e beam reach
  f in irons/no-sail zone
11 port tack
12 starboard tack
13 tacking
14 jibing
15 "Ready about," "Helm's a-lee"
16 "Prepare to jibe," "Jibe-ho"
17 trim, mainsail
18 wing, wing
19 sailing, lee
20 accidental jibe

SAILING DRILLS BUILD SAILING SKILLS page 88 answers

1 angle, wind
2
  a foot
  b luff
  c leech
3 draft
4 forward
5 boom vang
6 ease, luffing
7
  a ease, trim
  b head up, bear away
8 weather
9 lee
10
  a windward
  b head up
  c ease, sheet
  d traveler
11 reefing
12
  a Form a non-slipping loop, tie jibsheets to clew of jib
  b Keep line from slipping through fairlead or block
  c Tie two ends of a line together
  d Secure a dock line to a horn cleat
  e Temporary tie-up to dock piling, attach fenders to stanchion
  f More secure tie-up to dock piling
13 hove-to
14 jib, mainsail, helm (tiller)
15
  a bow line
  b stern line
  c forward spring
  d aft spring
16 fenders
17 close reach
18 a upwind approach

STEPS TO INDEPENDENT SAILING page 114 answers

1 sight, hearing
2 collision
3 stand-on, course
4 give-way
5 give way
6 starboard
7 windward
8 power-driven
9 give way, overtaking
10 neither, starboard
11 give way
12 early, substantial, stand-on
13 registered, documented
14 life jacket (or PFD), each
15 flares, smoke signals, distress flag, electric distress light
16 air horn
17 fire extinguisher
18 red, starboard, white
19 steaming
20 0.08
21 buoy, fixed
22 color, shape, number
23 "red right returning"
24 safe water
25
  a spotter
  b flotation
  c close reach
  d luffing
26 jibe
27 weather
28 float